February 2005

Dear Family and Friends,

We are excited and honored to share this new book with you in hope that both Christians and non-Christians will see Jesus Christ, His message, and the church in a simple yet profound and candid way. "The Truth You <u>Know</u> You Know" clearly reveals how all people bear the image of God, how divine truth is truly self-evident, how Jesus Christ breaks the cycle of cause and effect that is prevalent in all religions, and how westernized Christians have inadvertently turned many away from Jesus' message of hope. "The Truth You <u>Know</u> You Know" is written by Ken Rideout, a highly respected 44-year missionary to Thailand, and a dear friend whom we have known and supported for twenty five years. The freshness of Ken's message comes from his eastern perspective on western-minded Christian teaching, and he writes in the same way he taught in the East. Ken draws church-going Christians out of the box and enables the church-offended and non-Christians to see the hope of Jesus without the trappings of dogma. We hope to hear from you after you read this book. If it moves you to want to know more about Jesus, please call us. If it moves you to spread the fresh perspective, please buy a book and give it to a friend. We are excited for our friend but we are just as excited for the message he presents.

Sincerely,

Ron and Windy Warren

310-548-9069   wwwarren@sbcglobal.net

The Truth You <u>Know</u> You Know

Jesus Verified in Our Global Culture

N. Kenneth Rideout

by N. Kenneth Rideout

Copyright ©2005 N. Kenneth Rideout. All rights reserved.

This edition distributed by:

> NDX Press
> div. of Child Sensitive Communication, LLC
> PO Box 40269
> Nashville, TN 37204-0269
> 1-615-383-8845, www.ndxpress.com

Editor: Karyn Henley
Layout: Kristi J. West
Producer: Ralph Henley
Cover Photo: comstock.com. Used by permission.

All Scripture quotations, unless otherwise indicated, are taken from the NEW AMERICAN STANDARD BIBLE ©1960, 1962, 1963, 1968, 1971, 1972, 1973, 1975, 1977, by the Lockman Foundation. Used by permission.

Scriptures marked NIV quoted from the HOLY BIBLE, NEW INTERNATIONAL VERSION®. Copyright © 1973, 1978, 1984 by the International Bible Society. Used by permission of Zondervan Publishing House. All rights reserved.

Scriptures marked RSV quoted from THE REVISED STANDARD VERSION, Old Testament Section, © 1952; New Testament Section, First Edition, © 1946; Second Edition, © 1971 by the Division of Christian Education of the National Council of Churches of Christ in the United States of America. Used by permission.

Scriptures marked NRSV quoted from THE NEW REVISED STANDARD VERSION, © 1989 by the Division of Christian Education of the National Council of Churches of Christ in the United States of America. Used by permission.

Scriptures marked NKJV quoted from THE HOLY BIBLE, NEW KING JAMES VERSION © 1982 by Thomas Nelson, Inc. Used by permission.

"He Paid a Debt He Did Not Owe" w/m by Ellis J. Crum, Kendallville, IN, 1979.
Arr. © Copyright 1979 "Special Sacred Selections," by Ellis J. Crum, publisher; Kendallville, IN, 46755. International copyright secured. All rights reserved. All arrangements with these words or this theme are illegal unless authorized by owner.

No part of this publication may be reproduced, stored in a retrieval system, or transmitted in any form or by any means (electronic, mechanical, photocopying, recording, or otherwise) without prior written permission.

Printed in the U.S.A.

ISBN 0-9743197-9-1

> A free, down-loadable study guide is available online for those who want to use this book as a course of study. You can find it at: www.TheTruthYouKnowYouKnow.com

Table of Contents

Acknowledgement	v
Introduction	ix
Before You Read Further	xv

PART ONE — 1

1.	The Truth You Know You Know	3
2.	Truth: Two Languages and Two Dimensions	9
3.	The Image of God in Every Person	17
	Interlude: The Indonesian Banker	22
4.	The Blinding of the Human Heart	25
	Interlude: The Thai Village	34
5.	The Common Denominator	39
6.	The Wrath of the Law	53
	Recap to This Point	65
	Interlude: The Sheik and the Leper	67
7.	If Only There Were a Mediator	69
	Interlude: The True Story of the Tiger King and His Helmsman	84

8.	From Sons of Men to Sons of God	87
9.	Christ Unrealized and Christ Realized	97
10.	Identifying Christ in the Hearts of the World	103
	Interlude: Philosophies in a Nutshell	121
11.	The Equation of Faith	123

PART TWO   143

	Interlude: The Final Exam	145
12.	How Truth Verifies Itself	151
	Vignettes	168
13.	Cultural Barriers	171
	Interlude: Hill Tribal Village	182
14.	The Barriers WE Build	187
	Interlude: Discovering an Unknown God	209
15.	Telling What You Know You Know	211

| Appendix A: Further Reference Material | 221 |
| Appendix B: An Example of Witnessing Through Dialogue | 232 |

A Deep and Sincere Acknowledgement

I must acknowledge first and foremost my deepest eternal thanks to the God and Father of our Lord Jesus Christ and to His precious Holy Spirit Who empowers us with His Truth and Knowledge. From the very beginning of my life in Christ, the image of God has been the living source of all the knowledge I have gained and have put forth in this book. Beyond that, God has led me through the lives of thousands, and to all those many people from Asia and America I also feel a deep sense of gratitude.

God's presence has ever been a guiding reality to me. Always, it seems, God has spoken to me, not with an audible voice, but in the Spirit. As a child, I learned to talk continually to Him upon my bed or walking through the fields and woods. As silently as God leads a bear to mate, seek food, and train its cubs, as silently as God instructs birds to migrate, so the silent, mysterious intellect of God has always guided me. God has been the Source constantly illuminating my actions, and my own childish awareness of my sin has given witness to His holiness.

I have never felt myself to be one of God's great gifted ones, but I have always felt called and elected to desire Truth and Holiness before Him and all men. In this effort, I have felt most miserably inadequate. It is here, in my inherent weakness and in the innate frailty of my effort, that the grace of God's forgiving love and the sustaining imputation of His righteousness through Jesus Christ grips and holds me. I truly perceive God as immeasurable Love.

This life of learning began first with my parents, Albert and Mable Rideout. I acknowledge them to be my first teachers. They were filled with the Holy Spirit of Truth, and everyone who knew them could see their reverence for the heart of God and their belief in the Bible. My father and mother were generous people to those in need. Both were believers dedicated to honesty and industry, ready and able to share their faith as well as their goods, and they consistently did so. When I was about nine or ten years old, they accepted Jesus. At that point, they began instructing me in the belief they held so strongly. Their true witness of honesty, love, and generous service to others confirmed to me the witness of the Father's constant presence in their lives and in my life as well.

My first wife, Ruth Ann Bailey Rideout, taught me to be a godly man, husband, father, and lover of people. Without her unselfish and sweet spirit faithfully and patiently encouraging me through our 43 years together, I could never have written this book. Her death of cancer in 1994 was a deep loss, but God in His faithfulness had made provision. Sandra Womack Rideout, my second wife, is the loving and affectionate disciple in this effort. She is a tender-hearted prayer warrior with true godly faith. She has encouraged and assisted me to bring this book to completion.

I'm seventy-four now, and my teachers number in the hundreds. They have guided me through countless classroom hours and numerous books. Reference volumes and library periodicals have all chipped away at my rough, unbending ignorance. Conversations with godly professors about the grace of God have left me pondering truth through nights and over years. I must apologize for a lack of comprehensive acknowledgement of those who have taught me and have opened doors that set my mind and heart racing toward the growing beauty of God the Father. I simply cannot remember who all my teachers were, nor how each contributed to my understanding of God's love. How can I name all the men and women of a lifetime who have spoken and written the Truth of God's goodness and love? Among them are all the writers of the Old and New Testaments as well as Plato, Aristotle, Calvin, Luther, Karl Barth, Marcus Barth, Brunner, Bultmann, John Baillie, Donald Baillie, George McDonald, C.S. Lewis, Ralph Winter, Pat Hardeman, Donald McGavern, Peter Wagner, Charles Kraft, Oswald

Chambers, Norman Grubb, Pat Boone, and many others, all of whom have had lasting influence on me.

Finally, without the help of Karyn and Ralph Henley, this book would never have come to completion. Karyn, author of the original *The Beginner's Bible* and many other fine books for children, parents, and teachers, came alongside with her great talents for editing, rewriting, and simplifying an otherwise cumbersome text. She gave countless hours in this endeavor. Ralph proved an excellent resource with his ability to distill difficult concepts and to provide technical resources for getting the manuscript published. They have been invaluable, and I am deeply grateful for their encouragement and their patience in listening to me for hours on end.

When you read this book, you will know I have spent my life with people of many different races and beliefs. In each case, as I have been with them, I have been with the Lord. Devout men and women who are Buddhist, Animist, Confucian, Hindu, and Muslim have all helped to form me and expand my awareness of how immeasurable is the love of God in Jesus Christ. All of them have taught me precious Truth. And they have taught me to question. To them, and to all who love Truth and dare to rethink old positions in this grand pursuit to know the Lord and to reach the lost and hopeless with the blessed gospel of the God and Father of our Lord Jesus Christ, I dedicate this effort of a lifetime.

Ken Rideout
September 2004

INTRODUCTION

When I first arrived in Thailand over forty years ago, I thought the people would be hungry to learn about the love of God and His provision for salvation. Instead, I found that they had serious questions. One question surfaced in a class where I taught the book of John to 100 men from the University of Chulalongkhorn in Bangkok. These men were from the upper class and were some of the finest students in all of Thailand. That day, as I taught from John 3:16, a group of three or four young men in the back of the room sat laughing and talking among themselves. I asked them to share with us what was so funny.

One of the young men stood. I could see that he was on the offensive, which was quite unusual for a Thai student. It meant he did not really consider me to be his teacher. He said, "You foreigners travel 12,000 miles to tell us God loves us, God is love, Jesus is God's Son. You expect us to believe that Jesus raised the dead, walked on water, and did other miracles. Yet you tell us that if we do not believe your Jesus, we will die and perish forever, condemned by your God. Yours is just a narrow-minded religion. Our religion is broad. We do not condemn anyone. When we listen to you Christians, we see that some of you do not even believe that the other Christians are being saved. You condemn one another. We don't even know which missionary teaches the truth."

I realized then that what I had been telling the students had not enabled them to hear the love of God.

People would ask me, "Why do you believe that Jesus is God's Son?"

"The Bible teaches that He is," I would answer.

"Why do you believe the Bible?" they would ask.

Then I would discuss evidences the way I had been taught in the Western world. And I would think I was doing a good job. But when I finished, they still did not believe.

In my second year in Thailand, I taught a class of four nurses and two young men from the same university, one of whom was studying in the field of science. I had given them a survey from Genesis 1 all the way through to the second coming of Christ and the Judgment. Each time I asked if they had any questions, they had none.

At last, the young man studying science said, "You say God created the heavens and the earth and the first man and woman. God put the man and woman in the Garden of Eden, a paradise where there was no death and no sin. Then this Satan came and tempted them. Who created Satan? Where did he come from? Did God create Satan to tempt man? Then you say that because of this sin, death came upon the world, and the man and woman were cast out of the Garden of Eden. Wickedness and corruption came into the world. Then God sent Jesus to die for the sins of the people. All who believe on Jesus can be saved and go to heaven. All who do not believe will die condemned. You say heaven is a paradise. Will there be sin there, as there was in the paradise of Eden?"

"There will be no sin in heaven," I said. "For Satan and his angels will be destroyed."

"Why didn't God do that the first time, instead of leaving sin and wickedness, pain and torture in the world?" he asked. "You say that the masses of the world are going to perish under God's condemnation. What is God doing? Playing a game?"

My heart was troubled. My students could not hear the message of God's love. Instead, they heard exclusivism and condemnation: We are right and you are wrong; we are saved and you are lost; God is infinite love to us, but to two-thirds of the world's population, He is condemnation.

The Thai people saw that I lived a good, honest life. Country people even called me "khun chaub taam," which means "the righteous one." But the witness of my righteous life lost its converting strength because of the way I presented the gospel of Christ. What was supposed to be good news did not ring true to them.

After four years in Thailand, I came home to pursue a doctorate degree in the field of biblical studies. I wanted to learn about the ancient traditions and culture of the Middle East. Perhaps then I could understand how the gospel message, originally presented to Easterners, convinced them to become believers. I prayed, "Lord, give me a simple Mars Hill presentation." [1] Armed with new insights, I then returned to Thailand and spent 40 more years there, teaching about God and His love.

I recently returned to the United States, and what I found was a vastly changed society from the one I left 44 years earlier. Today in Western society, many Asian concepts of the spiritual and natural world have subtly permeated our thinking. Our society's world view is being reshaped by the influx of people from Asia and the Middle East along with their religious beliefs; the rise of New Age thinking; a growing hedonism and self absorption born of affluence; and global economics and communication. We have become a pluralistic society. Atheism has grown, and Christianity has become a point of attack. Millions of believers no longer attend church. The media and entertainment industry powerfully influence every area of our lives. Peoples' consciences have been seared to sin so that the problems sin creates—the destruction of homes, financial irresponsibility, increasing violence, declining moral values—have all become a way of life.

I also found that most Christians are not equipped to address these changing views in their witness to the gospel. All over the U.S., I have asked Christians, "Do you truly believe that Jesus is God in human form? He lived and walked upon the earth? He never sinned but lived a perfectly holy life such as only God could do? He was hung on a cross, died, and rose from death by the power of the Holy Spirit? As living Lord, He reigns in righteousness, bringing salvation and the hope of eternal life? You truly believe this? Prove it." When I say this, most Christians, even pastors, look at me with a stunned, blank expression. But that's what the world is demanding of us, and that's what it expects that we cannot do. If we cannot prove these answers for ourselves, how can we prove such things to others?

**You truly believe? Prove it.
That's what the world is demanding.**

With this book, I hope to lay a new set of tracks about how to present the good news of Jesus Christ in a way that speaks to the secular, the global, and the Eastern frame of reference. So in Part One, I will build a foundation for this approach. At times, this approach may sound dissonant to widely held concepts of what the Bible teaches. Some of what you read may shake your frame of reference or make you question my theology. But please keep reading, because Part Two will be practical, showing how to witness Christ to our current global culture. It is my hope that a full reading of this book will show the validity of this type of presentation. The fact is, we cannot walk through a closed, locked door. We must unlock and open the door to our global culture. What we say must be valid to people's hearts.

I assume that the person who has chosen to read this book is religious, has a good heart, believes in the moral law, and has a desire to learn and become more useful with his faith. That could generally describe a Christian who wants to witness vibrantly to the Eastern mind, the New Age adherent, and the disenchanted believer. How can you share the Good News in a way that will unlock and open the door of these hearts? I am hopeful that you will find the answer in the following pages. It is my desire that you be able to explain God's good news in a way that will allow it to unlock and open the doors of the hearts of unbelievers and the disenchanted, as well the hearts of your own children, so they will know what they believe and why.

---

[1] See Paul's discussion with the philosophers on Mars Hill, also called the Areopagus, in Athens, Acts 17:16-34.

The aim of this book
is to show how the love of God
verifies itself to the human heart,
so that when you see Jesus,
He corresponds to the truth
you know you know.

Before You Read Further

You will understand the following pages better if I briefly lay some groundwork for you.

Dialogue

The ancient method of pursuing truth was called dialogue, people bouncing ideas off each other until they reach truth. This method of learning, used by Socrates, Plato, Buddha, and even Jesus Himself, allows teacher and student to reason to truth. By dialoguing, teacher and student can discover truth together rather than relying on scholarship or documents or other external confirmation. In dialogue, simple conversations are built on propositions leading to conclusions which are true to the listener and to which he can heartily agree. I used this method quite effectively in my teaching in Asia. This is the method demonstrated in chapter one of this book, the account of my interactions at the University of Beijing Medical School. I will use this same method often throughout this book.

A Self-Verifying Apologetic

The defense of the gospel is called an apologetic. The book of Genesis is apologetic. Deuteronomy is apologetic. The gospel of John is apologetic. Romans and Hebrews are apologetic writings. The New Testament was written as its own presentation of the gospel of God in Jesus Christ. The thinking in this book returns to that original, biblical style of apologetics.

In the New Testament, the Holy Spirit of Truth is the method used to establish that God actually took on the image of man in order to reveal His loving heart and character to mankind. God's plan is that *the gospel message itself is self-verifying.* As the New Testament has done, we, in dialogue, will also do: *allow the Holy Spirit to verify Truth to the human heart.* Therefore, I minimize the use of scriptures as proof texts. This is deliberate, for I am adopting the methodology used by Jesus, the apostle Paul, and the other New Testament writers, all of whom proclaimed the gospel before the Bible existed as we know it.

Jesus and the New Testament writers also taught from the people's mindset. I want to enable you to follow their example and trust the Holy Spirit to confirm the message to the hearer's heart. I simply present the good news in dialogue with people, and the truth verifies itself to all, young and old, rich and poor, Buddhist, Hindu, Muslim, educated and uneducated, people out of every nation and religion.

Metonomy [1]

As you read, you will see that I often use a variety of terms to describe God's love and character. Just as we might examine a cut diamond, turning it to view many different facets, we can think about God and behold many different facets of His being, all of which are necessary aspects of His fullness and glory. In literary terms, using one aspect of something in order to refer to the whole thing itself is called metonymy. This is a common figure of speech, and we often see it used in reference to the names of God. God is:

Our righteousness

    Our peace

        Our holiness

           Our redemption

Each of these, from the human perspective, is only one aspect of God, yet each contains the sum total of all the others. For if we are to speak of God, we are limited to human terms for the unspeakable, the omnipotent, the One whose ways are higher than our ways and Who moves well beyond the scope of human effort to describe. God is One, indivisible, yet we know Him by different names or aspects, depending on the characteristics which we experience or try to describe at any given time. By using metonymy, we can take in the broad spectrum of God's immeasurable love.

So you might read something like:

> By grace we are saved.
>> By Christ we are saved.
>>> By the Holy Spirit we are saved.
>>>> By God we are saved.

Which is it? The answer is *all*. All these phrases amount to the same thing. When we try to speak of God and His absolute holiness and faithfulness, we have many choices as to how we might portray Him.

Problems can arise, however, when we try to describe the infinite in terms of the finite. Once we break down that which is total and complete into parts we can understand and discuss, it becomes easy to focus on the part and lose sight of the whole. Focusing on parts can lead us away from, rather than into, the whole Truth of God and His love through Jesus Christ. God is indivisible, but as finite humans, we can speak of God only in divisible terms, such as kindness, or righteousness, or forgiveness, or love. God is all of these, but not in the sense of one attribute added to the next to arrive at a total. With God we always multiply: One times one times one is still One. Righteousness times kindness times mercy is still God.

References to Buddhism

You will notice that most of the examples I use deal with Buddhism. This is because I lived and worked in Buddhist countries for 44 years. The Buddhist culture became my teacher in clarifying Eastern philosophy and has sparked my thinking in regard to presenting the message of Jesus in that context. So Buddhism has been the first and best-known of the Eastern religions to me, and is therefore a richer source for illustration and example.

Gender-Sensitive Words

Throughout this book, I refer to our own species, humans, in a variety of terms. As much as I can, I have used *mankind, people, human beings, person,* but there are places in the text where the word *man* in the neuter gender, meaning both male and female, was the best form of expression. It seemed too burdensome and stilted for colloquial American English to say in every instance *man and woman* or *him or her.* My heart is motivated by the New Testament admonition for "men and women to prefer one another in love." Superiority of any one of us over the other has no place in our hearts, as it has no place in God's heart. If this leading seems unsatisfactory, I can say only that I despise the exaltation of either man or woman above the other to their detriment.

I make the same accommodation in reference to God as He. God being God, He is not masculine, feminine, or neuter, and He must essentially be our Mother as well as our Father when we think in parental terms. I was preaching in southern India one time when, at the close of my talk, a Jainist priest raised his hand. "I really like what you are saying about this father in heaven," he said. "But you have not said anything about mother." We are so limited by language as we try to say what we truly mean. We can speak of God only with the language He has given us to express Him. "Father" does not mean that God has gender. It simply means progenitor, creator, protector, provider, and whatever else "father" can convey to his children. So I use the word "Father" in the common English usage. But I will never refer to God as "it." We cannot love an "it," because love is personal, and "it" is not personal.

---

[1] Metonymy, "Rhet. The use of the name of one object or concept for that of another to which it is related, or of which it is a part, as 'scepter' for 'sovereignty,' or 'the bottle' for 'strong drink' or 'count heads

(or noses)' for 'count people.'" <u>Webster's Encyclopedic Unabridged Dictionary of the English Language</u>, Gramercy Books, New York, 1989, s.v. "Metonymy."

PART ONE

CHAPTER ONE

The Truth You Know You Know

Beijing, Communist China
Summer, 1981

    A dry, burning breeze blew into the city from the Gobi Desert as I wove through crowds of people, all dressed in faded navy, gray, or black. I was making my way to the Beijing Medical University where I taught English. My class consisted of 50 doctors and nurses, both men and women, ages 32 to 60. These were some of China's most intelligent people. As such, they had endured much suffering during the destructive fury of the Cultural Revolution, which had spread death and cultural ruin throughout China. One of these doctors, described by the others as the best surgeon in China, had told me he had spent the last eight years walking the rice paddies barefooted. Another had said that the Red Guards had taken her husband and children away. She had not seen them for over ten years, nor did she know where they were even now.

    But by 1981, China was beginning to emerge onto the world stage from the bleakness and fear of the Cultural Revolution as a new leader attempted to bring the nation into an era of openness. Teams of English teachers from the West had been invited to upgrade education. So here I was in a hot, colorless city. The authorities, who knew I was a

Christian but not that I was a missionary, had said I would be allowed to give a Christian witness. But no public gatherings would be permitted.

With this knowledge, I entered my classroom each day and faced this special group of doctors and professors. Their white shirts and blouses were wrinkled. Their drab trousers and skirts were faded. On their feet, they wore rubber thongs or well-worn, unpolished leather shoes. Yet in spite of their humble clothing, they had a keen intellect and self-esteem. These amiable doctors and nurses possessed a wholesome respect for their station and accomplishments, and perceived their comrades to be compassionate benefactors of the Chinese.

I assumed that all my students were currently Communist, or had been in the past, for they had spent their lives under atheistic communism. Religious witnessing had been forbidden, and Christians had been marked as ignorant and primitive. In fact, just a few years earlier, learning English or even showing any Western skills with music would have resulted in death or imprisonment. But now the Chinese were being encouraged to study English. They were allowed to question Westerners freely, so they were full of questions, endlessly asking about everything. It seemed that their curiosity about me was never quenched.

One day, one of the doctors asked, "How do you prove God?"

"You do not prove God," I said. "You *know* God. We prove things in the physical world by experimenting with measurements, weights, chemicals, heat, light, and so on. But you cannot put God in a test tube or measure His dimensions. God is Spirit. Things of the Spirit dimension need no proving, because God's Spirit bears witness to our spirits. God's Spirit confirms the truth of His love and His being."

After some silent thought, the doctors said, "We don't understand."

"Should you lie, rob, murder, or cheat me?" I asked. "Should you take my wife by force? Should you rape my daughter?"

"No!" they answered.

"Are you sure?" I asked.

"Yes," they all said. "We are sure."

"Prove it," I said. "Prove that these things are wrong."

Everyone was silent.

"I agree with you," I said. "We all agree that these things are wrong. I am an American, and you are Chinese. Our language, culture, and political systems are different. Yet on this most important issue for relationship among all people, we agree. There is no need to prove it, for we all know it. It is a self-evident truth, universally understood. Things of the Spirit need no proof, for our Maker has written His image of love and moral righteousness upon every human heart. All over the world, regardless of nation, language, or creed, men and women, adults and children, educated and uneducated, all alike know that such behavior is bad. Each person knows what is good."

Things of the Spirit need no proof.
Our Maker has written His image of love and moral righteousness
upon every human heart.

Then I asked another question. "If I love you so deeply that I would die for you, would I lie, rob, murder, cheat, or mistreat you in any way?"

"No," they said. "You wouldn't."

I placed one of my index fingers over the other, forming a cross. "If I loved you like this, so that I would die for you after you put nails into my hands and feet, pierced my side with a sword, or pressed a crown of sharp thorns into my brow, would I ever murder or rob or cheat you?"

Without hesitation, they said, "No."

"Do you have to prove that?" I asked.

Again they answered, "No."

"What kind of a world would it be if we all loved each other with such love?" I asked.

"It would be a great world," they said.

Love fulfills all moral and ethical responsibilities toward one another.

"We all know that it would be a great world if we loved each other with the love our Creator has given us," I said. "We believe it, because it is true. God has put within us the knowledge of His love. Whoever our Maker is, He has made us with a common knowledge: Love fulfills all moral and ethical responsibilities toward one another. We do not have to prove it; we know it. This kind of love implies the personal. That's why we say, 'God is love, and love is personal.'"

Love That Proves to be True

This explanation of God's love, which the Chinese doctors pondered that day, is so simple that a little child can easily understand it. Yet it is also profound. We believe God is love, because He has written the truth of His love in the hearts of all people. We not only feel love, but we also see it when people are kind and compassionate toward us. This love is the absolute of mankind's ability to exist in self-fulfillment and in personal relationships. Its multiple facets hold all that distinguishes us as both relational and rational human beings. We know we must love truth, morality, humanity, integrity, responsibility, honor, respect, righteousness, and life — our own as well as others'. To the human heart, such love continually proves itself to be true.

Summary: Chapter 1

You don't have to prove God; you know God.
All people agree on basic universal moral law.
Perfect love fulfills the whole moral law.
This kind of love is personal.
The highest description of God is Perfect Love.
God is personal.

CHAPTER TWO

Truth: Two Languages and Two Dimensions

We all seek to know truth. It would be rather difficult to find someone who says he has no concern for truth. Such a person would not be worthy of trust. He would not stand for anything. He could not be the president of a college or the principal of a high school or the governor of a state. He would be distrusted. Scientists, paleontologists, astronomers, chemists, all seek truth. Truth is that to which men give their lives. It is truth upon which men stand. Truth overrides personal likes and dislikes. And it is truth to which we are all responsible. It is truth that we seek.

Two Languages of Truth

We use *truth* in both a secondary sense and a primary sense. For example, I say, "This is a table." I knock on it with my fist and find that it's hard. That's true. It conforms to the fact of the matter. I see that the table is brown. That's also true. But it is not truth in the spiritual dimension. The descriptions of the table are factual truths, but none of those facts has permanency. So this kind of truth is the secondary, external truth that we see in the natural dimension; a truth we feel, smell, and taste; a truth of the corruptible and temporary.

The earth on which we live had a definite beginning and will have an end. There is a knowledge of this world, a wisdom of this world, a light of this world. But the world and all things in it are passing away. Eastern thought calls it an illusion. So this kind of light, wisdom, and knowledge has no eternal value. It is corruptible and temporary. In contrast, spiritual truth, or the true reality, is an eternal dimension and does not change. There is a Knowledge, a Wisdom, a Light that does not pass away. This permanence is found only in the primary, eternal truth of the spiritual world. God is eternal Truth, and this world is a changing illusion.

Spiritual truth is an eternal dimension and does not change.

Hinduism, Buddhism, Judaism, and the Greek philosophers all spoke about real truth as something other than this earthly dimension. They recognized that we are in a changing world, so they spoke of this world as not being *real*. For example, the Greek Stoic philosophers saw this world as an illusion. As early as 540-475 B.C., Heraclites taught that the world was changing and impermanent. He said a person cannot put his foot in the same river twice, because the water he stepped into has gone by the time he takes his foot out. By the same logic, it is not the same foot. Some of the cells have died and fallen off. The foot is older, if only by moments.

Gautama Buddha, contemporary with the Greek philosopher Heraclites, lived in India from 563-483 B.C., and taught that the world was a changing illusion. He, like Heraclites, believed that everything was in constant flux. Buddhism states, "All is matter; all is physical." In that physical realm, nothing stays the same. We in the West now know that this is scientifically correct. The table looks solid, but it is made of atoms and molecules banging around. So in reality, it is constantly changing.

Plato taught that there is a real world that is permanent and unchanging, but that the world we live in is impermanent and changing, a reflection, a shadow of the real. He found a counterpart for everything: life in this shadow world, life in the reality world. So we talk about the table; that is true. We breathe air; that is true. But none of that is the truth that is eternal, permanent, and unchanging.

God is eternal Truth, and this world is a changing illusion.

In both Greek and Eastern thought, philosophers acknowledged that there are two dimensions of truth: the seen and the unseen, a physical and a spiritual world. The physical is in constant change, but the spiritual is eternal reality, the truth that does not change. When we acknowledge our belief in God, we acknowledge these two dimensions. God is Spirit, and the world is physical. We have truth of the Spirit that is unchanging, and we have factual truth, the physical that is always changing.

Two Dimensions of Truth in the New Testament

Understanding the concept of two dimensions gives clarity to the New Testament. When Jesus said, "I am the Truth," [1] and "My kingdom is not of this world," [2] He was saying, "I am the Reality, not of this world, but of another world." In other words, Truth is not of this world. The apostle Paul writes about Jesus, " . . . who, being in very nature God, did not consider equality with God something to be grasped, but made himself nothing, taking the very nature of a servant, being made in human likeness." [3] Jesus was in the realm of the True, the Reality, the Something, and came into that which is the nothing, the physical world of humanity.

Paul wrote clearly about the two dimensions: " . . . what is seen is temporary, but what is unseen is eternal." [4] He wrote about the inner man and the outer man, stating that the outer man is a changing, temporal, passing truth, but the inner man is eternal. So in the context of his day, which included Greek and Eastern philosophy, Paul agrees with the philosophers, except he says the Reality is God, who is the Something, and it is the world that is nothing. Why did Paul write this way? Because the people to whom he wrote understood that reality existed in two dimensions.

The New Testament clearly states that the "form of this world is passing away." [5] But God is eternal. He does not change. When James wrote, ". . . from the Father of lights from whom there is no shadow cast by turning," he was talking about the reality world, not the reflection. [6] Greeks understood what James was saying, because they generally believed that this world was simply the shadow of a reality world.

So there are two dimensions. One dimension is the truth of this world, a body of information, a compendium of facts that has no eternal value. But when we say God is True, we are speaking of another dimension.

Mankind has known about these two dimensions since time began. "In the beginning God created the heavens and the earth." [7] This simple opening statement of the Bible sets the framework for understanding the existence of two dimensions, which are clearly set in contrast to one another:

<u>GOD</u>	<u>THE WORLD</u>
Creator	creation
Heaven	earth
Spirit	matter
Life	death
Eternal	temporal
Grace	law
Light	darkness

The Verification of Truth

So Truth is a matter of the spirit and not of the natural world. Philosophers from both the Western and Eastern world have understood exactly what every Asian person knows and says: Everything is changing.

- But does Truth change? No.
- Are you changing? Yes. You are not the same person who sat down to read a few minutes ago. You are growing older as you read this. So you are not the Truth.
- Is the chair in which you sit changing? Yes. It is wearing out as you sit in it. So it is not the Truth.
- Are you and I together the Truth? No. So the church is not the Truth. Nor are human institutions.
- Does the world change? Yes. So this world and its natural phenomena are not the Truth.
- Does the form in which Truth is expressed change? Yes. So our forms — the Sabbath, circumcision, baptism, communion are not the Truth. Churches and relationships break up over the observation of these rites. But these are not eternal values. They are only ceremony and ritual, forms used to express Truth. Truth transcends what we describe as religious behavior.

Truth is a matter of the spirit and not of the natural world.

As we saw earlier, the primary, but not exclusive, authentication of spiritual Truth is the Spirit of Truth. Though God chose to reveal His Truth and heart through physical man, the confirmation of His Truth is never what the eye sees or what physical data may prove. Instead, the confirmation is always God's Spirit bearing witness with man's spirit,

Some may say, "There is no truth." To that, I would ask, Is that true?" interpreting what the eye sees and the ear hears. God knows our heart and character, because He has written Himself upon our hearts so that we may know Him as He knows us. God has given His Holy Spirit of Truth to witness to us according to His scheme in creation.

The scriptures of the New Testament are another witness of the Spirit of Truth. But what we read there is not true simply because it is in the Bible. On the contrary, it is in the Bible because it is Truth. Truth was Truth before the Bible was written. Truth has existed since *before* the beginning of time. Adam knew Truth. Noah knew Truth. Abraham, Isaac, and Jacob knew Truth before scripture was ever written.

Scripture is not true simply because it is in the Bible. On the contrary, it is in the Bible because it is Truth.

Truth is above and beyond man. The Eternal Truth may use a man to communicate Truth, but the hearer looks past the man and listens to see if the message corresponds to the inward truth within his own heart. In fact, the messenger may fail to live the Truth he proclaims, but if he does, he can be set aside. Yet the Truth he has spoken remains. So it is that Truth itself is always the witness, even to the one proclaiming it.

Throughout this book then, Truth with a capital T signifies the spiritual dimension, a realm not proved by instruments of science nor established by facts of history. God is not proved by physical tools. He is known in the context of the spirit, and He has made it possible to identify Him with spiritual tools. So the two dimensions must not be confused. Truth is the spiritual dimension. Outside of God, there is no Truth.

Proof resides in the heart of every man
in the form of an eternal, unchanging, intangible Truth.

Does God exist, and can you prove it? That was the question posed by the Chinese doctors. The answer is that proof resides in the heart of every man in the form of an eternal, unchanging, intangible Truth that is simple and easy to understand.

The Truth verifies itself.
It's just that way.

Summary: Chapter 2

There are two dimensions expressed in two languages:
    One of this world, factual with no eternal value.
    One of the spiritual world: True Reality, unchanging, eternal.
Truth does not change.
God is Spirit, eternal, unchanging.
God is Truth.
The knowledge of the physical world is proved by scientific facts.
The spiritual world is a knowledge of the heart.
The Truth verifies itself to the heart.

1 John 14:6
2 John 18:36
3 Philippians 2:6-7, NIV
4 2 Corinthians 4:18, NIV
   First Corinthians 1 and 2 are a dynamic argument for these two dimensions.
5 1 John 2:17
6 James 1:17
7 Genesis 1:1, NIV

CHAPTER THREE

The Image of God in Every Person

*"And God created man in His own image,...
and breathed into his nostrils the breath of life,
and man became a living being."*
Genesis 1:27, 2:7, NIV

*All created things are but the word of God
in manifest form, good and beautiful.*
— Norman Grubb

Darkness lay upon the face of the earth. God made the heavenly bodies and the earthly forms. Yet there was no awareness of God. Not in the trees. Not in the rocks. Beauty was not perceived as beauty. The giving of love was not complete, for love is life and awareness. The greatest thing God could do was to make creatures who incarnated, embodied, His love. So God made man, and wrote within man's heart His love; love that had freedom; love that had creative power. This was the crowning act of His glory of creation: making a being who bore His image.

When God did this, He placed the identical image of love in all human beings of all races, creeds, beliefs, and nationalities. He has not put a different image into the Hindu from the image He placed in the African animist or the Northern European Christian. We have all been created with one identical image: God's. This identity unifies humanity and establishes the universal ground of Truth that we all know. Among all human beings, God's image of love becomes the common denominator for identifying Truth and for validating His heart and character to each of us.

Love, as described to the Chinese doctors, expresses the totality of man's uniqueness compared to all other creatures. We are rational beings who, at our very core, know that love binds people together: mother with child, husband with wife, neighbor with neighbor in community. Love, placed in us by our Maker, is the common denominator, the common image, the common moral Truth among all people.

**Love is the common denominator,
the common image,
the common moral Truth among all people.**

Springing from this image within, people perceive the universal Truth that it is morally wrong to murder one's neighbor, take his wife, or rape his daughter. Why is this universally understood? Because moral Truth resides within human beings, reflecting the image of our divine Maker and His nature of love. And because moral Truth is personal and rational and regulates human relationships, we can identify in our Maker these same divine qualities, which are fulfilled in love.

Innate Knowledge

God, by creating people in His image, has placed in each heart a knowledge of Himself. This knowledge is incarnate within each person. Therefore all people know love: God's love, which is deeper than what a mother or a father or an environment has taught. God is love, and His image of love pervades the very nature of mankind.

Thus the response of the Chinese doctors shows how love verifies itself to the human heart. They readily accepted the assertion that love fulfills the whole moral law. These doctors heard a message of love, reached down into their own hearts, and confirmed that it was true.

> CARNAL *means "flesh."*
> INCARNATE *means "In the flesh."*
> *To say that this knowledge is incarnate means that God has written it into our very being.*

Even though they had lived in an atheistic, communist regime for most of their lives, love found self-verification in their hearts, because of the image within them. The same knowledge is incarnate within all people, so that the good news of a loving God and Father finds self-verification in the human heart. No one needs to prove the message, because the Spirit of God bears witness to the image of God within man, confirming that it is true. God is Spirit and He is Truth; Truth that is not abstract, but personal.

We don't have to grope for God. We don't have to seek Him in some far off place. We are made in His image so that we may know Him. The Greek philosophers perceived this Truth. In fact, the apostle Paul reasoned from their philosophy and quoted them: "He is not far from each one of us. 'For in Him we live and move and have our being.' As even some of your own poets have said, 'We are His offspring.'" [1]

In the Hebrew letter, we read that God ". . .spoke long ago to the fathers in the prophets in many portions and in many ways. . ." [2] These prophets have been not only Hebrew prophets or even those traditionally accepted as "God's people." God also spoke through King Cyrus and through Balaam. He spoke to Nebuchadnezzar in dreams. He spoke to the Roman centurion, the Syro-Phoenician woman, the ten lepers, Cornelius, and the Samaritan woman. In this way, their "copy" of the image of God and His love became the ground for verifying the Truth and character of God to them.

God created man as a rational being, so it stands to reason that He stays in relationship and communication with what He created. In the words of George MacDonald, a nineteenth century writer:

> If there be a God at all, it is absurd to suppose that his ways of working should be such as to destroy his side of the highest relation that can exist.... I mean, the relation of the will of the Creator to the individual will of his creature. [3]

This is the nature of love. God's image is the common denominator from which God can communicate with us. In this way, God's word is always "living and active, sharper than any two-edged sword, piercing until it divides soul from spirit, joints from marrow; it is able to judge the thoughts and intentions of the heart." [4]

Within each heart, God's image is always the rule of thumb for our relationship to one another. All mankind knows that if we reach out, touch, console, understand, or bear a burden, we express the love confirmed as moral Truth by the Chinese doctors. Even if people make no appeal to a God entity, they have to admit that if there were a God, the most important Truth would be that God loves them and that there is hope for mankind. We do not have to prove this. It is just that way.

**God's image is always the rule of thumb
for our relationship to one another.**

Our Maker has not left us without a vibrant witness of Himself. Every human being knows the love that dwells in him by the image of God. This is the incarnation of the knowledge of God that makes us all one and enables us to communicate from a common denominator, a common standard: His image within.

Summary: Chapter 3

Our Creator placed His nature of love in all people,
   His image in all people,
   A knowledge of Himself in all people.
So all people know love.
This is an incarnate knowledge.
God's image is the common denominator from which God can
   communicate with us.
We are all one family with one Father.
This Truth verifies itself to the heart.

---

[1] Acts 17:28, NIV

[2] Hebrews 1:1

[3] Harry Verploegh, comp., <u>3000 Quotations from the Writings of George MacDonald</u> (Grand Rapids: Revell, 1996) 111.

[4] Hebrews 4:12, NRSV

Interlude

The Indonesian Banker

Jakarta, Indonesia
1965

At a meeting I held one time in Kuala Lumpur, some prominent citizens from the Chinese business and government community in Malaysia became Christians. Not long after that, they sent me with a note to a friend of theirs who was the director of the Overseas Chinese Bank in Indonesia. The note said, "Ken has taught us a truth, and we wish you would listen to what he has to say." So the bank director scheduled a luncheon meeting with me and provided me with his car and chauffeur so I might see the city until time for our luncheon engagement.

At noon, we met at a restaurant. After we were seated, the banker asked, "What is this truth my friends wrote about?"

I asked, "Do you believe in God?"

"No," he replied.

"Why?" I asked.

"I have lived a long time and have seen a lot in this world," he said. "I have seen killings, wars, endless injustices, cruelty. Right outside the door of this restaurant, people do not have enough food to eat, and here we sit in luxury, enjoying ourselves. If there were a God, he would not create or tolerate a world like this. Therefore, there is not a God. If there were a God, he would not be worthy of my respect."

I took a piece of paper and drew a line down the middle, making two columns. On the left, I wrote "The World" and listed the ills for which the banker had accused God. On the other side, I wrote "God."

Pointing to the chart, I repeated what he had just said, blaming God for allowing these terrible situations to exist in the world.

The World		God
Adultery		
Lying	Rape	
Cheating	War	
Murder	Cruelty	

"Let us say that there is no God." I quickly drew an X through God's name in the right column. "Has anything changed now that we have taken God out of the picture?"

"No," he said.

"Without God in the picture, who is to blame for the evil that is in the world: the lying, cheating, murder, adultery, rape, war, and so forth?" I asked.

The World		~~God~~
Adultery		Man
Lying	Rape	
Cheating	War	
Murder	Cruelty	

"Man," he said.

I wrote "Man" in the right column under the crossed-out "God."

"Why blame man for all this?" I asked. "Why hold him responsible? The tiger eats the deer. The cat eats the mouse. The landslide wipes out an entire village. Why do we not blame the tiger, cat, and landslide in the same way we blame man?"

"Because man is a responsible being with a will," said the banker.

"He chooses his actions."

"Are you sure man is responsible?" I asked.

"Yes," he said.

"So let us put God back in the picture," I said. "Why blame God for what you say man has freely chosen to do?"

The discussion went on from there. It was not until 20 years later that one night, about midnight, with three of his friends from Kuala Lumpur, this Indonesian banker confessed that he needed the love of God as revealed in Jesus Christ.

The non-Christian, the atheist, and the agnostic consistently deny the existence of God or blame Him for the state the world is in. Yet, as this wealthy Chinese banker had to admit, the problem is really man.

A friend of mine who owns a small mechanic shop has a saying pasted on the front of his computer: "Dear God, I have only one problem — it's me."

CHAPTER FOUR

The Blinding of the Human Heart

> Now the serpent was more crafty than any beast of the field which the Lord God had made. And he said to the woman, "Indeed, has God said, 'You shall not eat from any tree of the garden'?" And the woman said to the serpent, "From the fruit of the trees of the garden we may eat; but from the fruit of the tree which is in the middle of the garden, God has said, 'You shall not eat from it or touch it, lest you die.'" And the serpent said to the woman, "You surely shall not die! For God knows that in the day you eat from it your eyes will be opened, and you will be like God, knowing good and evil." When the woman saw that the tree was good for food, and that it was a delight to the eyes, and that the tree was desirable to make one wise, she took from its fruit and ate; and she gave also to her husband with her, and he ate. Then the eyes of both of them were opened . . . And they heard the sound of the Lord God walking in the garden in the cool of the day, and the man and his wife hid themselves from the presence of the Lord God among the trees of the garden. Then the Lord God called to the man, and said to him, "Where are you?" And he said, "I heard the sound of Thee in the garden, and I was afraid . . ." And He said, "Have you eaten from the tree of which I commanded you not to eat?" And the man said, "The woman whom Thou gavest to be with me, she gave me from the tree, and I ate."
>
> Genesis 3:1-12

> How has it happened that a God of love
> has come to be viewed as a God of wrath?

This story of man's fall yields one of the most profound insights into how and why man is in constant confusion in a world that is morally and environmentally corrupt. Man introduced sin through disobedience. When he did, he felt the full force of the law and its judgment. Then in his own mind, he distorted God's heart and character into wrath. How has it happened that a God of love who has put His image of love within us has come to be viewed as a God of wrath? How has "the god of this world. . .blinded the minds of the unbelieving"? [1] The Genesis 3 account tells us.

Man's First Perception of God as Wrathful

There are three very important universal truths in this account of Adam and Eve:

"There is no fear in love. But perfect love casts out fear, because fear involves punishment." [2]

"For the Law brings about wrath; but where there is no Law, neither is there violation." [3]

It is sin that blinds. And "the power of sin is the law." [4]

When God left Adam and Eve in the morning, they had a loving relationship with their Maker, because there was no fear. By the time God returned in the cool of the day, that relationship had changed. But who had changed? Not God. He was still the same loving, merciful, good Creator that He had been that morning. What had changed was the man and woman's perception of God. They now had a law relationship with God. And since the law brings wrath, they perceived God as wrathful.

Adam and Eve were ashamed and afraid. Why? They had been disobedient. Now their Maker was returning. The moment of Truth had come. They had to face God.

It wasn't just that they had eaten forbidden fruit. It was what the eating of the fruit represented. Eve's goal was to be like God, which in itself is not a bad desire. It was an innocent aim that unconsciously created a new self-image, displacing the perfect love God had given man and woman when He placed His image within them. Eve assumed that becoming like God could be derived from the creation. That was the first idolatry, the first act of unbelief.

Man and woman chose to have an image in opposition to God: "My will against your will." They were now violators of the law written on their hearts when God first created them. Although they still lived in the Garden, its beauty dimmed because of their shame and fear. Just as a rainy day can seem beautiful to the heart that is full of goodness and joy, or the sunny day can seem burdensome to one full of sin and shame, the problem lies in the condition of the heart.

Even though Adam and Eve bore God's image and lived in Paradise, they could no longer perceive God as being perfectly loving and good. Their new knowledge of good and evil had revealed the existence of the law that God had placed in all of creation. And they were now under the power of that law, with sin in dominion over them. They knew that what they had done deserved punishment. What they had sown, they would have to reap. This is how "the law brings wrath." Adam and Eve could see no such thing as grace and forgiveness. Assuming that God could not forgive, they became afraid of Him. For "fear has to do with punishment." So in the evening, they ran and hid. Blindness had descended over their hearts. Adam and Eve's awareness of sin had distorted their view of God, blinding their minds to His love and glory.

Now the concept of the "wrath of God" began to grow within Adam and Eve. They knew they had not lived up to God's perfect beauty, love, and goodness. So instead of sensing love as the essence of God's heart and character, they saw God as angry and unforgiving. They perceived God through the law, which they now realized was a result of failing to reflect His glory. Their personal relationship with God was replaced by relationship with law. The moment they fell into shame and fear before God, the moment of sin, they lost their position, and they lost paradise. Law became the mediator between God and man. But it was a mediator that could bring only wrath.

Law became the mediator between God and man.

Then the law of sin and death, as it always does, multiplied sin. After Genesis 3, people still had God's image in them, still knew the good they should do, and taught their children and neighbors, "Do good." But they could not cease from evil. Instead, they invented new ways to sin. By the time we finish the book of Genesis, mankind is already experiencing murder, envy, war, jealousy, revenge, hatred, slavery, racial and national partiality, and more. If people experienced a little sin, then they experienced a little wrath and saw God as angry. But when their sin was great, they saw God as a tyrant. It thus became unthinkable to consider Him as a personal God.

The Learning Process

Did God know that human beings would sin? Yes. The fall of man was the logical consequence of the image of God being put into man. When God decided to create man in His image, rational and personally aware of His love, God understood that man would sin. God's love nature required that man have the right to control his own thoughts, intentions, and decisions. He placed the tree of the knowledge of good and evil in the garden of Eden. Then he told man to do whatever he wanted, except eat from that tree.

How did God know that man would sin? Simply because man is not God. When God decided to put the knowledge of His infinite love in man, He knew that no one could live up to that love perfectly. Man is the creation and not the Creator. It is a simple fact that man can never live all the time being as perfectly good as His Maker. Even good people who seek to do what's right are weak and cannot escape their own sin. Humans continually miss the mark, never able to live up to the image of love within them.

When God decided to create man in His image, God understood that man would sin.

God, of course, does not sin. He is love, grace, mercy, and forgiveness. But these terms have meaning only when they are compared to sin, transgression, and disobedience. How do people come to know the gracious, merciful, forgiving heart of God? By going through a learning process to acquire a knowledge of good and evil. The tree was a symbol necessary to the intellectual and spiritual growth of man. It educated man so he could understand the goodness of God.

God knew that man would sin, and He takes responsibility for it. His purpose was that we would learn that we are not God, and that then we would allow Him to be God, the Supreme Creator.

Our Own Loss of Innocence

The Genesis 3 story corresponds to each of our lives. It serves to remind us of how we all came to have the knowledge of good and evil. It is the story of the entire human race. The ancient tree of the knowledge of good and evil has not faded away, but remains in our hearts to this day. We all, like Adam and Eve, have eaten from this ancient tree of worldly wisdom and have lost our innocence. The age, time, place, and circumstance of when we partook of this forbidden fruit varies with us all. I don't know when, where, or how it happened to me. I know only that I have eaten of it. At that moment, my youthful relationship with God changed. I don't remember exactly when shame, guilt, and fear began. I know only that I have experienced these feelings, and they are justifiable. I am a sinner. This I dare not deny. Since all sin is against God, I feel responsible to God, just as Adam and Eve did. The law of human nature has established the knowledge of the good that I ought to do and has created the guilt that arises when I don't do it.

We, like Adam and Eve, have experienced this awakening to life and have gained an awareness of God. We, like they, have "heard" His voice. We have known the nearness of His footsteps. And, like Adam and Eve, we have experienced God's departure from our presence, only to find that He appears after we have desired the forbidden fruit and have eaten of it. Upon every disobedience on our part, we have found our eyes opened, only to realize that we have experienced the awareness of good and evil.

This is not a one-time occurrence. Each time we sin, we come to know good and evil as God knows it, but we do not become the God that He is. Instead, He departs, and we become more aware of how habitually we turn to listen to the serpent. Yet, even though God has departed, His absence stirs us to turn and see Him beckoning.

The relationship between God and man is like any relationship. It has two versions: how God sees it and how man sees it. The account of the fall of man in Genesis 3 is above all a lesson about how we perceive our relationship to God and His relationship to us. God's name and image are written on every heart. But each person's perception of God defines the relationship. It may be warm and loving. It may be cold and rejecting. It may be a polite philosophical conversation piece. In any case, there is no way to escape a personal relationship with God.

The Genesis 3 story speaks eternal Truth to our hearts. God is personal. Choose God, and you choose a fellowship of grace and reconciliation. Reject God, and you place yourself under law and violate your true human nature.

Law always brings wrath. But no such attribute resides in God. In reality, we perceive God's displeasure and interpret it as anger. But we cannot speak truthfully about God's anger in the same way that we say we have anger, for human anger and wrath is associated with pride. It's true that the ancients spoke of the "wrath and anger" of God, but the perception of such wrath and anger is possible only when God is viewed through law.

**People experience the wrath of the law,
but blame God for it.**

The power of sin is the law, and that law distorts the image of God in the eyes of the one who has sinned. [5] Law is a fearful thing when violated, for it exacts wrath, associating wrongdoing with punishment. This is a principle accepted all over the world. All cultures and religions know the law of sowing and reaping: If you do good, you receive good; if you do evil, you receive evil.

Just as the Chinese doctors knew, all people know: Whoever our

Maker is, He has instilled in all of His creation a common moral law, a principle of cause and effect that is fully intended to bring abundant life. Instead, it brings death. In the following chapter, we shall begin to understand why.

Summary: Chapter 4

In the beginning, man had a loving relationship with God.
Man introduced sin
> by disobedience to God's image.
> by violating the loving image within his heart.
> by setting up a new self-image.

Man could no longer perceive God's love.
Man had a new knowledge of good and evil.
Man now perceived the existence of law in creation.
Knowing law, man came under its power because of sin.
Law's cause and effect means no escape from sin's consequences.
Through law, man saw God as angry and unforgiving.
A relationship of law replaced a relationship of love with God.
Law became a condemning mediator.
God knew this would happen when He placed His image in man.
> Because the creation is not the Creator.
> Because the creation cannot live up to the image of love within.

Through sin, man learned that he is not God.

1. 2 Corinthians 4:4
2. 1 John 4:18
3. Romans 4:15
4. 1 Corinthians 15:56
5. 1 Corinthians 15:56

INTERLUDE

The Thai Village

"Hello, hello everybody," I sing as I enter a Thai village. "Are you well? Is there anything you want that I may help you with?"

The Thais are friendly people. They come out to greet us. First come the shy, giggling children, followed by women and men. We laugh and joke and play.

Then they ask, "Why have you come?"

"I have great news for you," I say.

"What news?" they ask.

I tell them to gather the children and stand them in front of me, for this is news I want children to hear as well as adults. The older children, accustomed to attending school, stand there waiting to be taught. The younger children, naked and dirty, join them.

"Children," I say, "the God who made all the earth and the heavens and the distant stars loves you. Is that good news?"

"Yes," they answer quickly.

I turn to the parents. "Did you teach them this?"

"No," say the parents.

I turn back to the children. "The God who made all the heavens and earth loves you so much He wants to forgive you of all your sins, so that you can be holy and pure and perfectly good and go live with him in heaven forever and ever. Is that good news?"

"Yes," they say.

Again I turn to the parents. "How do they know this? Did you teach them this?"

The adults laugh. "No," they say. "We did not teach this."

"The God who made the heavens and earth loves you so much He wants to be your father and take you to live with him forever and ever. Is that good news?"

A third time, the children say, "Yes!"

A third time, I turn to the parents. "Did you teach them this?"

"No," they say, smiling.

I then ask the children, "Should you lie to me, murder me, steal from me, and cheat me out of what I have?"

"No," the children immediately answer.

"Should I be kind and merciful? Should I love you and forgive you of any sins you may do against me?"

"Yes," they say.

"Have you ever sinned?" I ask.

Most of them say, "Yes." Some of the young ones say they have never sinned. So I ask if they've ever hit anyone in anger or if they've ever taken anything that they shouldn't have taken from a brother or sister. They say, "Yes."

So I ask, "Is that sin?"

The young ones laugh with embarrassment and say that it is sin. All the children, as well as the adults, laugh at the thought that the young ones would say they have never sinned.

Then I ask the children, "If you do good, you get. . .what?"

"GOOD!" they shout.

"If you do evil, must you reap that evil?" I ask.

"Yes," they say.

"So if you sin, must it be punished?"

"Yes."

This is a cardinal teaching in Buddhism: As you sow, so shall you reap. There is no forgiveness of sins. All are under the law of nature, a cause and effect principle. There is a corresponding effect for every cause. There is no escape from this cycle.

"Will money take away the evil?" I ask. "Will education take away your sins? If you rob and kill somebody, will doing a good act take away that sin?"

"No!" say the children.

"So when you die, you die in your sins. You take your sins with you. Is that true or false?" I ask.

They say it's true.

"Is sin for heaven or hell?" I ask.

"Hell," they answer. They know this, because Buddhism teaches that there is a type of hell.

"Can sin go to heaven and be with God in His holy and pure place?"

"No," say the children.

Once again, I turn to the parents. I ask if they taught their children these truths. They reply as before. They have not. So I brag on their children and say how smart these children are. The adults laugh.

I ask the children. "If we die in our sins, where are we going? To heaven or to hell?"

This time, no one answers. They laugh and stare at me. But they know. They feel the impact of the question, and so do the parents.

I say, "The good news is that God, who has made the law of sowing and reaping, has also fulfilled the law. He loves us so much that He gave His only Son, so that whoever believes on Him need not perish. Is that good news?"

"YES," they say. "That is good news."

"Suppose people do not know about God's love for them. When that happens, they are not under the power and blessings of God's love. In their hearts and minds they know that they are now under the power of the cause and effect of the law of nature. What does the law of nature teach? It teaches us that we are born, grow old, get sick, and die." The children chant this last sentence with me, because it's a

Buddhist phrase, and it's very familiar to them. "Is that good news?"

"No-o-o-o," say the children.

"The law of nature is not good news to us," I say. "The law of nature teaches us, our human nature, to do good, do good, do good. Is that true?"

"Yes," say the children.

"Can you do it?"

"No," they say.

"The problem is that no one does the good!"

The children laugh as well as the parents. They laugh, because they know it's true.

"Will the law of nature forgive our sins?"

"No."

"Can money or education or philosophy forgive our sins?"

"No."

"Under the law of nature, we must die in our sins. We know we are going to hell. Is this good news?"

"No," they say.

"Which is better: to be under the law of nature in which you do good with no knowledge of where you are going, or to be under the love of God? Which is the good news?"

All the children say, "The love of God."

The Truth You Know You Know

CHAPTER FIVE

The Common Denominator

> *"For when [Gentiles] who do not have the Law do instinctively the things of the Law, these, not having the Law, are the Law unto themselves; in that they show the work of the Law written in their hearts, their conscience bearing witness, and their thoughts alternately accusing or else defending them."*
>
> Romans 2:14, 15

Paradise was lost in the hearts of Adam and Eve at the moment of their sin. They became lawbreakers and feared punishment. A shift had happened. The image of love in their hearts had been overshadowed by an awareness of a system that had existed from the beginning: law. Before Adam and Eve became aware of good and evil, before they became aware that recompense must follow every good and evil deed, God had put the entire universe under the function of cause and effect. Cause and effect is law. So law existed by means of Creation itself. Adam and Eve simply became aware of it when they sinned. Their eyes were opened to law.

Piglets, Water Lilies, and Light

When my wife and I were raising our family in Thailand, I decided my children should have the experience of seeing piglets being born. So one day I stopped by a pig farm operated by the Thai government. "Do you have any sows due to give birth soon?" I asked.

"Oh, yes," the farmer said. "There should be some piglets born this evening."

So that evening, I took my children to the pig farm. Our timing was good. It wasn't long before the sow we were watching birthed her piglets. As soon as each piglet was born, it would crawl down and around the sow's foot, over her huge back legs, toward her teats. One by one, the little pigs made their way straight to their mother's milk.

"Daddy, how do they know which way to go?" my children asked.

"That's a good question," I said.

We asked the Thai farmer, "How do newborn piglets know how to get to the teats?"

"The law of nature," said the farmer. He was a poor, simple man, yet he understood what everyone knows: All of creation is controlled and ordered by law, the cause and effect principle operating within the nature of anything to bring about a predetermined end. So everything within nature follows the law of its own nature, whether it is animal, plant, or human. As scientists know, those laws can be discovered, documented, and predicted.

**All of creation is controlled and ordered by law,
the cause and effect principle operating within the nature of anything
to bring about a predetermined end.**

Newborn piglets follow the law of their nature to find nourishment. But the law of nature for a pig is different from the law of nature for a fish, because the law of any part of the natural world is defined by its nature. In other words, the law of anything is written within the thing itself. For example, the law of the water lily is defined by the nature of the water lily. If you plant a water lily in dirt as if it were a rose, it dies. But if you plant a water lily in water, it thrives.

The law of anything is written within the thing itself.

For as long as people have existed, they have been discovering and cataloguing these laws of nature. To discover the law of something is to understand how it works. For example, in order to understand how light works, scientists study light under a variety of circumstances. They observe light's cause and effect, and describe their discoveries as the law that regulates light. Knowing that the law of light is predictable allows us to use light and organize our lives according to its nature. Another example is in the area of medicine. Doctors know by observing cause and effect that if they do one thing, the patient gets well. If they do another, the patient remains sick. We observe another function of law when astronauts travel into space. Space travel is possible only because through the centuries, scientific observation and documentation has produced a sufficient understanding of the laws of aerodynamics.

Everything in the world operates according to its own law of nature.

Laws control the whole creation. Laws establish harmony and prevent chaos. Laws give predictability to all things, because law is causational. That is, once there is a cause, a corresponding effect must follow. If the stem of the apple breaks loose from the branch, the apple must fall. By the same law of gravity, if a man jumps off a cliff, his jump will be the cause that will result in an immediate and deadly effect. Isaac Newton's well-known Third Law of Motion states that every action causes an equal and opposite reaction, clearly showing the cause and effect relationship of the physical world.

Natural law is the common denominator that no one can escape. We are taught by it. We are controlled by it. We depend upon it. It is unthinkable to try to change it. The law of nature willingly gives up its truth to the searching mind. "Discover me," it seems to say, "and use me to your good or to your hurt. Change me you cannot."

Once known, law can be accepted or ignored in human action. When ignored, a law of nature metes out its own consequence. Human beings thus cannot "make" a law. The only thing man can do is introduce his acquired knowledge or discovery of how law works. Newton and other scientists did not make any laws of physics or chemistry; they just discovered them.

The Law of Human Nature

The law of human nature can be expressed in relation to human action as well, which means that the law at work in human nature is also predictable. Moral law operates in the same way as the law in the physical world, that is, by the principle of cause and effect. People reap what they sow. The awareness of this Truth has been the predominant denominator in the physical as well as the spiritual/psychological realm of mankind throughout the ages. What philosophers from ancient times to the present have dis-covered is the natural moral law that God has written on the hearts of all people.

We speak of LAW in the singular and LAWS in the plural. We use LAWS in the plural, because there are many things with different natures. LAW in the singular carries a broad but simple meaning: the CAUSE AND EFFECT PRINCIPLE.

**The philosophies and religions of the world
derive their moral judgments
by discovering the laws of human nature.**

When I went to Asia, I thought I had to teach people the moral law: Don't lie, murder, or steal. But I learned that Buddhism has been teaching morality for 2500 years. The moral law is not known to only one group of people while remaining unknown to another. Nor is this moral law a code exclusively inscribed in certain books. Buddhism, Taoism, Confucianism, and Hinduism have been teaching "do good, do good, do good" for thousands of years.

The Buddhist explains it this way: "The Law of cause and effect includes not only the laws of physics and chemistry so familiar to the Western world; it also includes laws of moral or psychological cause and effect known as... 'karma.'" [1] So when applied to human action, the law of nature expresses itself as:

    Law of Sowing and Reaping
        Law of Works
             Law of Karma
                  Universal Moral Law.

Just as physical laws are not made but discovered, so also moral law is discovered. The philosophies and religions of the world, without exception, derive their moral judgments by discovering the laws of human nature. Again, Buddhism is a good example.

> To the Buddhists, the universe is a cosmos
> under the reign of Law and whatever happens is
> a detail in an unending chain of cause and
> effect. The gods are as subject to this law as

> men. It holds good equally in the moral sphere and in the physical. Every wrong deed or word, every evil thought must work out its results, its effect and that of its own force quite independently of any duty. It is absolutely impossible for a conscious being to escape this result of his own act or thought, or. . . his karma. [2]

So the law of karma (the law of works) is simply a discovered principle of cause and effect in human action. Buddhism stresses the doing of good in deed and in thought. It advocates the eradication of all greed, hatred, and egotism from one's mind. It urges the cultivation and development of compassion, sympathetic joy, and equanimity as inherent aspects of one's personality.

> "Hatred ceases not by hatred in this world. Through love it comes to an end. This is an ancient law." "Overcome anger by love, evil by good. Conquer the greedy with liberality and with truth the speaker of falsehoods." [3] "Buddhism . . . can give a complete explanation of its moral principles and in fact all of the teachings of the Buddha because they are based upon universal laws which are unchangeable and which represent the absolute truth." [4]

I have used Buddhism as an illustration, because I spent so many years in Thailand. However, these observations are not uniquely Buddhist. They also find expression in the other philosophies and religions of the world. For example, contemporary to Buddha in the sixth century B.C., Greek philosophers developed the concept of the Logos. Heraclites used the term *Logos* to describe a divine force that produces the order and pattern discernible in the flux of nature. Later the Stoics depicted the Logos as a rational divine power that not only orders, but also directs the universe. They identified the Logos with God, nature, and fate, and spoke of the Logos as being present everywhere. To the Stoic:

> "True divine law is to be sought only in the cosmos, where one law rules that is the basis of society and the union of divine and human beings. As reason, this law pervades nature and determines moral conduct." [5]

Later, the Romans used the Greek philosophical ideas to develop their own principles of the moral law:

> True law is right reason in agreement with Nature; it is of universal application, unchanging and everlasting; it summons to duty by its commands and averts from wrongdoing by its prohibitions. . . .There will not be different laws at Rome and at Athens, or different laws now and in the future, but one eternal and unchangeable law will be valid for all times. And there will be one common master and ruler of men, that is God, who is the author, interpreter and proposer of this law. Whoever will not obey it is trying to escape from himself, and in denying the true nature of man he will thereby suffer the severest penalties, even if he escapes what is commonly considered punishment. [6]

The Chinese Confucian philosopher Mencius, considered the cofounder of Confucianism, also taught principles of cause and effect. He traveled for years, teaching these principles and telling rulers about their lawful duties toward their subjects. To Mencius, it was a self-evident truth that the feelings of commiseration, shame, courtesy, and right and wrong are all inborn in humans. These feelings are cultivated into the virtues of benevolence, righteousness, propriety, and moral consciousness, which are within humans from their origin. [7]

> **The writings of all ancient philosophies and religions establish the fact that there is a universal moral law.**

Ancient philosophies and religions establish in their writings the fact that there is a universal moral law. But no matter what a religion calls the law its originators discovered, under that law, mercy cannot reign supreme. Why? Because law requires recompense. Law itself can never forgive. The effect must follow the cause. As we saw earlier, "It is absolutely impossible for a conscious being to escape this result of his own act or thought, or. . . his karma." [8]

God and the Law

It is not only human beings who must conform to the law. God Himself conforms to the law. But notice: The relationship of God and the Law does not imply obedience. And the word *Law* here does not mean civil law. As it applies to God, *Law* has two aspects. The first is that of the natural moral Law which God has written on the hearts of all people, which is Perfect Love, His image, His nature, our standard. For God, His nature is not something for Him to obey, but is simply the expression of Himself, which humans sense as the standard of goodness, honesty, respect, compassion, and all qualities of Perfect Love to which we aspire.

The second aspect of *Law* as it relates to God is the principle of cause and effect. This principle is at work on God's love. When He loves, His love has a loving effect. He is not obeying *Law* set up for Himself. He is acting in accordance with His nature. Throughout the rest of this book then, when the term *Law* is capitalized, it will mean the definition of Law or karma: the cause and effect <u>principle</u>, and not civil laws or codes of conduct.

Because Law is God's nature (the behavioral standard of perfect love) and is also the cause and effect principle precipitated by loving acts reaping the consequence of loving effects, God Himself conforms to the Law. The cause and effect principle cannot be repealed or destroyed, not even by the Lawgiver Himself. He cannot be partial. Otherwise, he would be a tyrant. Every good and evil deed must receive its reward. [9] For God to arbitrarily go outside the Law in order to forgive lawbreakers would make Him unjust. He would lose His moral integrity.

People of all cultures understand this about God and Law. D.T. Suzuki, the great Zen Buddhist, wrote:

> As far as phenomena existence are concerned, this law of cause and effect holds universally valid. Nothing, even God, can interfere in the course of things thus regulated, materially as well as normally. If God really exists and has some concern about our worldly affairs, he must first conform himself to the law of causation. [10]

Plato reasoned that if gods don't accept Law, they "corrupt their divinity" and have no right to be called gods. "Hence belief in God and justice rests on the *nomos* (Law)." [11] God can be considered just only insofar as the Law is fulfilled or satisfied. He will not violate the Law. *But He can fulfill it.*

When Law is the Common Denominator

As we have seen, when man lost paradise and his heart became blinded to God's glory and love, the image of God within man was overshadowed by the knowledge of good and evil, the experiential knowledge of Law. God intended for His own image, the guiding force of love, to be evidenced by man's loving actions. But when the relationship between God and man ceased to be motivated by love, man turned to selfish desires, and man's view of love became corrupted. Man became a lawbreaker. Therefore, civil law became necessary so that people could live at peace with one another.

Laws, as most of us think of them, arose to ensure that humanity would live up to God's image within man. In all societies, lawmakers reached down into their hearts to draw out principles of justice, mercy, and fairness to govern the actions of human beings in relationship. They codified these principles as "positive law" or "civil law." Legal systems and governments arose to administer these codes, of necessity using punishment, power, and intimidation to make people's actions conform to the righteousness and love of the inward image.

Around 1700 B.C., Hammurabi carved his governing codes on stone. Later, Moses gave the Israelites the Ten Commandments, which have become a foundation for codes of law in Western nations. Around 600 B.C., by the same knowledge of this inward, universal Law, the Buddhists established their *Five Precepts of Right Conduct*:

> Do not kill.
>> Do not steal.
>>> Do not lie.
>>>> Do not be unchaste.
>>>>> Do not take intoxicants. [12]

All humanity recognizes and esteems honesty, unselfish love, and the pursuit of good, not evil. But in reality, legislated codes cannot perform the very thing they are created to do. Legislation cannot change the heart. It can only try to control behavior. In all creation, Law is at work to hold all things in order and to keep the universe from chaos. Religions, philosophies, and societies of humanity recognize this, though they may speak of Law in different terms:

    Law of Nature
        Law of Cause and Effect
            Natural Law
                Law of Works or Sowing and Reaping
                    Law of Karma
                        Universal Moral Law

Throughout this book, these terms may be used interchangeably as Law is applied in various situations: human behavior, the workings of the physical world, and the relationship between God and His creation.

Paul echoes these various descriptions of Law in his writings in the New Testament. He speaks variously of

    the Law of God
        the Law of Christ
            the Law written in the heart
                the Law of works
                    the Law of Sin and Death
                      the Law of Moses
                          the Law of faith
                              the Law of the spirit of Life
                                  the Law of governments.

When man sinned, he became aware of his own human nature. He realized that to love as God is love was an impossible task for a human being. This awareness of his own nature brought with it an awareness of Law, the realization that humans must reap the effects of their actions. So from the moment each of us partakes of the forbidden fruit, Law reigns in our hearts. As creatures springing from Adam, we of necessity will sin. We will miss the mark. As a result, Law reigns over life, and sin has dominion over us. That is the common denominator. As the Thai children knew, the reign of Law is not good news, *because the Law does not forgive sins*. People must reap what they sow. It is the Law. And the Law brings wrath. [13]

Summary: Chapter 5

Law is the cause and effect principle that operates within the nature of anything to bring about a predetermined end.

Natural law

    exists by means of creation itself.

    is the function of cause and effect within the physical universe.

    operates within the physical world to keep order.

    cannot be escaped.

The Law of human nature operates in the same way.

    Effect must always follow cause.

    People must reap what they sow.

    The Law cannot extend mercy or forgive.

Cause and effect in human action is called the Law of karma.

This moral Law is in all people through God's image.

1 Chom Sookparimat, Buddhism: The Religion in Thailand (Bangkok: Choom Noom Chang) 1966, 2.
2 Encyclopedia of Religion and Ethics, s.v. "Buddhism," 1955 ed.
3 Dhammapada 5 and 223 as quoted in Buddhism: The Religion in Thailand, 6.
4 Dr. Luan Siryapong, Buddhism in the Light of Modern Scientific Ideas, 6, 7.
5 Gerhard Kittel, ed., The Theological Dictionary of the New Testament, vol. IV (Grand Rapids: Eerdmans) 85.
6 Cicero, De Republica,100-60 B.C.
7 John B. Noss, Man's Religions, 3rd ed. (New York: Macmillan, 1963) 404.
8 Encyclopedia of Religion and Ethics, s.v. "Buddhism," 1955 ed.
9 Hebrews 2:2
10 D. T. Suzuki, The Essence of Buddhism (London: The Buddhist Society, 1957).
11 Kittel's, Vol. 4. "Nomos" (W. Gutbrod, H. Kleinknecht)
12 The following are the five precepts of Buddhism, paraphrased from: Bhikku Khantipalo, Buddhism Explained: An Introduction to the Teachings of Lord Buddha (Bangkok: Mahamkut Rajavidyalaya Press, 1989), 193.

In parentheses beside each precept is the corresponding commandment from Exodus 20 in the Bible.
1. I will refrain from destroying life. (Do not kill.)
2. I will refrain from taking what is not given. (Do not steal.)
3. I will refrain from wrong-doing in sexual desires. (Do not commit adultery.)
4. I will refrain from false speech, that is lies, backbiting, harsh speech, and idle chatting. (Do not lie.)
5. I will refrain from distilled and fermented intoxicants which produce heedlessness.

13 Romans 4:15

CHAPTER SIX

The Wrath of Law

*"For the law brings wrath,
but where there is no law there is no transgression."*
Romans 4:15, RSV

The "Wrath of God" is the Law

Natural moral Law is universally perceived as "holy and just and good." Could God give anything less than a perfect Law? The Jewish scriptures confirmed over and over again that the law of Moses was faultless. Buddhists say that all the teachings of the Buddha ". . .are based upon universal laws which are unchangeable and which represent the absolute truth." [1] Yet the Law, being *impersonal* and impassionate, was never designed to forgive sin or provide grace and mercy. Instead, it was intended to be a tutor, a schoolmaster to bring people to grace, forgiveness, and mercy, attributes that are beyond the nature of the Law.

The Law, being *impersonal* , was never designed to forgive or provide grace and mercy. Instead, it was intended to bring people to grace, forgiveness, and mercy.

Remember: When man disobeyed the holy, just, and good commands, he realized that the cause — sin — required an effect — punishment. So he experienced the wrath of the Law. But he perceived God as the giver of the wrath that was actually imposed by the Law.

Man knew that his own heart held love. And he knew that the Law demanded that he exhibit the traits of love: forgiveness, patience, kindness. All the while, he was blind to the loving nature and forgiveness of God. So man began to exalt himself above God. Man knew that he himself could do something the Law could not do: love and forgive. In effect, man said, "I have patience and mercy. But God does not. I am the one who loves. God is condemning and wrathful." Having the very life of God within his bosom, man accused and rejected Him. Perceiving God to be a tyrant, man concluded that God must be impersonal.

The problem is one of perspective. If God exists, then mankind perceives Him as exhibiting wrath through judgment and punishment. If there is *no* God, or if there is only an *impersonal* God, then the issue is merely one of the outworking of Law, an unpleasant effect experienced as the result of an evil action. Man's actions, because of Law's causational impact, result in effects that are not judgments or condemnations, but the predetermined outworking, pleasant or unpleasant, of his deeds (karma). Eastern philosophy and religion resist speaking of sin, punishment, condemnation, or judgment, because these words all imply a personal God. They speak rather of worthy and unworthy actions and pleasant and unpleasant effects, which result from Law's causational operation upon human actions. This effect is not a judgment or punishment, but merely an outworking of the deed done.

**It is not God who brings wrath.
Wrath belongs to Law.**

"But God *is* wrathful," someone may say. "He is angry at us because we sin, isn't He? To say God is not wrathful would be doing away with punishment of sin, wouldn't it? If we take away the wrath of God, aren't we agreeing with those who say there is no sin and no punishment?"

The answer is simple. It is impossible to do away with wrath, God or no God. For wrath is the result of the working of the Law of karma (the Law of works). But it is not God who brings wrath. Wrath belongs to Law. Yet Law is perfect. The imperfection lies with man's inability to keep it. We experience wrath from the causational effect of Law upon our own evil deeds. If we do evil, Law demands that we get evil in return. There is no escape from this fact of the Law of cause and effect. In reality, the only hope for mercy and perfection lies with God.

No Escape from Law

The Law's purpose is to give life, for the whole world is made up of life. People, animals, and even plants exhibit a yearning to live. Even the Thai children knew that the requirements of the Law — kindness, mercy, love, and forgiveness — were right, for all of these bring abundant life. Moral Law does not exist to destroy people's self-image or life in human community. Instead, moral Law teaches us to love, be kind, good, understanding, and just, all of which are the greatest concepts in human thought.

God is called "the Judge." But that doesn't mean He is angry or wrathful. No court wants a judge who is wrathful, but one who is good and upright.

However, Law with no teeth is no law at all. Law enables people to reason logically when deciding what is evil and what is good. So Law is the criterion that demands justice against the evildoer and a correspon-ding reward for doing good. Upon the basis of natural moral Law, we are aware of the sins of Genghis Khan, Joseph Stalin, Adolph Hitler, Napoleon, Saddam Hussein, and Osama bin Laden. Law is the universal order that demands that such men be condemned and punished for the slaughter of untold millions.

People may reject God, but they cannot reject the Law of cause and effect working upon their nature, because God has written the Law in every person's heart. So in doing away with God, people put themselves under Law alone. And Law has no mercy. A person may not want to be judged by a personal God. He may say there is no God, therefore no sin, but he still knows in his heart, however he defines it, that there is good and evil, and that he can choose to do either. Whichever he does, he will reap an effect, now and ultimately. Without God, there is no escape from that fact.

**People may reject God,
but they cannot reject the Law of cause and effect.**

So whether a person says there is a God or not, it makes little difference to the Law. The person who believes in God thinks of the Law and its punishment for sin as an act of God. But if a person denies God, there is still punishment, which he perceives as an unpleasant effect. Nothing changes regarding a just recompense for every deed done. The only thing that changes is vocabulary. The person may say, "What goes around comes around." Or "Garbage in, garbage out." However he says it, Law is
> sowing and reaping,
>> cause and effect,
>>> impersonal,
>>>> impassionate,
>>>>> impartial,
>>>>>> the condemnation of evil.

Law cannot mediate in man's favor because of mankind's persistence in sin. In Eastern vocabulary, there is no way to escape from the outworking of the Law.

**Under Law,
the only thing that changes if a person denies God
is vocabulary.**

But something else happens when people reject what they see as a wrathful God: They automatically set themselves on a pedestal as if they themselves were God. The irony is that even when people see themselves as the highest being, they still acknowledge compassion, goodness, and love: the Law. And the very fact that people try to be loving, compassionate, and good on their own shows that they agree that the Law is right. People pass civil codes or positive laws and then set themselves up as judges in order to punish the evildoer, insisting, "It is not me judging you, but the law you have broken." What they will not allow God to do, they themselves do in the name of law. [2]

**Since no one can keep the Law perfectly,
everyone stands condemned.**

However, the cause and effect nature of Law produces an eye for eye, tooth for tooth mentality. Therefore, since no one can keep the Law perfectly, everyone stands condemned. Everyone will pay the consequence. Whether a person violates physical law or moral Law, the ultimate consequence of the violation of Law is death. Life must be snuffed out, and all that is within the world — all awareness, all compassion, all love — must be destroyed. Life lived under the Law of

nature follows the pattern that the Buddhists describe with their chant:
> You are born.
>> You get old.
>>> You get sick.
>>>> You die. 3

For those who live under Law, death is victorious over life.

Our Dilemma

Keeping the moral Law brings ultimate happiness, because the Law's purpose is to bring life. Not keeping the moral Law brings despair, because it leads to death. The "sting of death is sin, and the power of sin is the law," says Paul. 4 Therefore, because no one can meet the demands of the Law, the adherents of all religions live with the despair of trying to "do good, do good, do good," but not being able to keep the Law in spite of their best efforts.

People's hope is that death will end this dilemma in spite of all the evil they have done. They hope that somehow God will set aside the Law with its condemnation. Yet even in death, people cannot escape the cause and effect principle of Law. Dr. Luan Siryapong, author of <u>Buddhism in the Light of Modern Scientific Ideas</u> wrote, "Whatever karma (action) has been committed must inevitably run its natural course until the effects of his will-actions have exhausted themselves which may occur either in this life or in some future existence." 5 The apostle Paul wrote, "Do not be deceived, God is not mocked; for whatever a man sows, this he will also reap." 6

Every philosophy or religion that reasons using natural Law believes in some form of existence beyond the grave in order to resolve the Law's demands regarding the effects of sin. Reincarnation and rebirth, resurrection, heaven and hell have all been variously comprehended as logical consequences. 7 Everyone knows that sooner or later, a person must reap his own karma, because evil and sin can never be reconciled with the love and holiness of God.

Wrath and vengeance are totally incompatible with who God is.

There is no partnership between good and evil. But all people embody both and are at one moment good, and the next, evil. The apostle Paul expressed a dilemma that is impossible for philosophy or religion to solve: If we would all follow and obey this moral Law that we know, we would have the peace and joy we desire. Yet we do not always obey it. When we disobey, that same Law becomes our condemnation. Paul wrote:

> I find then a law, that evil is present with me, the one who wills to do good. For I delight in the law of God according to the inward man. But I see another law in my members, warring against the law of my mind, and bringing me into captivity to the law of sin which is in my members. O wretched man that I am! Who will deliver me from this body of death? I thank God through Jesus Christ our Lord! So then, with the mind I myself serve the law of God, but with the flesh the law of sin. [8]

The Law promises to give life. Its purpose is life. In fact, the Law is not anything other than God's Spirit, intellect, and reason controlling all things. For what sums up the requirements of the whole Law? Love. *If we love perfectly like God, we will fulfill every requirement of the Law.* But if we do not love, we have violated the whole Law. Then that which is meant to bring us love and life only succeeds in bringing us death, because we cannot live up to the Law, the standard set by God's Spirit, intellect, and reason. So God has given us something we cannot do:

> live up to His Image
> His love
> His righteousness
> His holiness.

Why can't we do this? Because we are the creation, not the Creator. We can never be God. When we sin, we are doing what comes naturally to us.

God knows this. He has always known that we cannot keep the Law. However, to say that God created the world and mankind, then put them under judgment and condemnation actually maligns God. Whenever we speak of God, we must always depict Him as being the loving, caring, compassionate, and merciful God that He is. It does not glorify God to say that He is full of wrath and vengeance. Though God is fully aware of these qualities in mankind, that does not mean that these are part of His character. In fact, wrath and vengeance are totally incompatible with who God is.

Why Does the Bible Speak of the Wrath of God?

If wrath and vengeance are not part of God's character, then why is it that the Old Testament speaks of the wrath of God, the anger of God, and the vengeance of God?

In the time of the Old Testament, sin had dominion over everyone, because the entire world was under Law, not grace. Being by nature sinners, when people came to God through Law, they perceived Him as wrathful, then wrote and spoke of Him as being angry and vengeful.

> In the time of the Old Testament,
> the entire world was under Law, not grace.

Just as the Jews approached God through Law, so did *all* the world until the Law was fulfilled in Christ. Thus the New Testament has far fewer references to God's wrath. When the New Testament writers did speak of the wrath, anger, and vengeance of God, they were referring to those who viewed the world through Law, perceived God as angry, and experienced Him as wrathful.

Many Christian scholars explain that God's anger and wrath isn't like ours, with evil intent or lack of control. It doesn't matter how it's explained, as long as people know that God is not a God of anger and vengeance. He foreknew that His creation would never perfectly keep His Law. He knew we would sin. And His love demanded that He not leave the world under the condemnation of Law. It is rational to think that God would scheme and plan redemption from that wrath for His creation. The wisdom of God is His love, and the great beneficiary of His love is us.

> God's love requires that He not leave the world
> under the condemnation of Law.
> God knew we would sin,
> and He had a plan.

Summary: Chapter 6

When man sinned, he experienced the wrath of the Law.
But man perceived God as wrathful because of Law's cause and effect:
>If you do good, you get good.
>If you do evil, you get evil.

Law teaches "do good, be merciful, be kind."
>So Law was intended to give life.

Law demands a just reward for deeds done.
Because all sin, all stand condemned.
>So Law brings death.

What was meant for life brings death.
>Law cannot mediate for the lawbreaker.
>That's why some see rebirth as necessary.

Because of Law's condemnation, God seems vengeful.
But God is neither vengeful nor angry.
God knew we would sin.
His love demanded that He provide a way out of the dilemma.

1 Chom Sookparimat, <u>Buddhism: The Religion in Thailand</u> (Bangkok: Choom Noom Chang) 1966, 3.

2 See Romans 7:10-16.

3 Buddhism says that self must be extinguished like a flame on a candle; Nirvana is complete absence of all that is the changing, illusory dimension. The Hindu states that all is God or all is Brahman and self is illusory, for down deep, the reality of God is there; the little self must cease by the realization of the SELF, so that all are God. Paul supports a true understanding very well in Romans 7:7-25.

4 1 Corinthians 15:56, NIV

5 Dr. Luan Siryapong, <u>Buddhism in the Light of Modern Scientific Ideas</u> (Bangkok: Mahamagutrad UP, 1954).

6 Galatians 6:7

7 Greeks, Egyptians, Hindus, Buddhists, and Asian philosophers all taught that reincarnation or rebirth were necessary. Persian religions and Jewish Pharisees believed in the resurrection of the dead even before the time of Jesus.

8 Romans 7:21-25, NKJV

Recap to This Point

God is Love
>In creating mankind, our Maker put His love into our hearts.
>Therefore, the image of God within mankind is His love.
>The image of God is in every person.
>It is the same image, whether a person is Hindu, African, native American, or any other culture, ethnicity, or philosophy.
>This common image of God means that God's love is also in the hearts of all people.
>It is universally understood that a common moral Law is also written on people's hearts.
>The moral Law is fulfilled by God's love placed in our hearts.
>If love is given by God, the Maker, then God is love.
>The nature of love is to give life.
>Love is personal.
>Therefore, God is personal.
>Without God and His love manifest in Jesus, there is only impersonal Law.
>Love is able to forgive violations of the moral Law, demonstrating that love is greater than the Law and will not violate the moral Law.
>Love is forgiving; therefore if God is love, God's forgiveness fulfills the Law.
>When man sinned, the knowledge of good and evil brought the fear of punishment.
>Man's relationship with God changed from a loving relationship to a wrathful relationship when viewed through Law.
>Man, with knowledge of good and evil, sees God only through Law.
>Law itself is just and holy and good.
>Therefore, the Law demands that man do good.

- The Law is meant to bring life, but it brings death, because man is unable to keep the Law perfectly.
- Law itself is incapable of forgiving, therefore man loses sight of the forgiveness, grace, and mercy of God.
- Under Law, there is no escape from the cycle of sowing and reaping, cause and effect of human action.
- Efforts to find an escape through reincarnation or rebirth have not solved the problem.
- Philosophies and religions have long known the need for a mediator to reach the essence of an unreachable God and His love.
- God knew before the foundation of the world that His created beings, bearing His image, would face this dilemma.

These conclusions come first by an understanding of the moral Law, which we all have in common. Second, they come from understanding that perfect, unselfish love fulfills the moral Law. Third, they come from knowing that love, like the moral Law, is designed to bring abundant life. These truths do not need to be proved. They are self-verifying, literally written upon the human heart.

Interlude

The Sheik and the Leper

Imagine a husband and wife, both lepers. They have eight children. The whole family is begging and trying to eke out an existence from discarded waste. They are shunned as "untouchables." Now a lordly sheik rides past on his ornamented elephant, attended by royalty and nobility wearing the finest of clothing. This sheik and his attendants are known for their selfish cruelty in their lordship over the people. They would never think of stopping to help the lepers.

As the lepers watch the sheik and his attendants ride past, they wonder, "Why were we born poor and leprous while this cruel group are wealthy rulers?"

Ancient philosophers and religious leaders, good hearts who were trying to be righteous, sought to explain these kinds of inequities. How could God truly be God and allow the world to be in such a state? Different explanations emerged around the world, but they all had a common thread. In the Greek world as well as in Eastern philosophies from India to China, that thread was reincarnation.

Here is how these philosophers would have answered the lepers: "We all are our karma. We came from our karma. We will be our karma. We cannot escape our karma. You are a poor leper, suffering and shameful, because in your former life, you committed terrible crimes. But this sheik inherited his wealth because of his former karma. Do not be dismayed, because in his next life, he will surely receive the evil karma that he is doing now."

While this explains the leper's poverty and the sheik's prosperity, it does nothing to relieve the leper's misery or to motivate the sheik to use his wealth to alleviate suffering. Each is reaping what he has sown in a former life, and each has no choice but to live out the effects of his karma.

To the leper, there was a gulf between him and the rich sheik, a chasm that could not be bridged. He thought he was hopelessly trapped by the Law of cause and effect, the karmic cycle of birth and rebirth. Who could bridge the gap? Who could cross the chasm? The lowly could never have come up to the high position. In order to bridge the gulf, the one in the high position would have had to come down to raise the lowly.

This is a prophetic parable that foresees what God must do to solve the dilemma of Law and sin and death. The sheik, though he was rich, would have had to become poor if his millions of lowly subjects were to share his wealth. This is what God would have to do. For God to be God, He would have to so mediate in the physical and spiritual.

***

It takes a man to mediate for man.
It takes God to mediate for God.

***

CHAPTER SEVEN

If Only There Were a Mediator

> *"The problem with the teaching of the Christian religion is that no one can keep it. It is too demanding and perfect in its requirements."* This is what a Chinese man said to me years ago when I first arrived in Hong Kong. I said, "You're right. That's why we need grace."

The Dilemma of Law and Grace

If we were to declare that there is no moral Law, we could comfortably ignore sin and say it does not exist. Yet the knowledge of good and evil that exists innately within every person is a natural Law for us and exerts its power over us. Its lesson is this: Don't violate the Law written upon your heart. It is holy and just and good. Obey it. Love perfectly. Yet we cannot obey it. We cannot love perfectly. That is the dilemma. What's more, the Law extends no grace, by nature being unable to forgive. All religions and philosophies know this fact.

All people bear identically an image they cannot live up to,
    a nature they cannot honor,
        a Law they cannot keep,
            a light they cannot sustain,
                a love they cannot fulfill.

Even so, people keep reaching for the greatest and highest. That is what the image of God requires of us, what the moral Law demands. There is no greater satisfaction to a person than to lie down at night, knowing he has accomplished something of beauty, truth, and righteousness; in other words, to know he has satisfied the demand of the moral Law, the Law of love.

> Whoever keeps the Law perfectly
> reigns supreme over the Law;
> Law no longer reigns supreme over him.

The whole aim of Law is toward that which fulfills it: love. Whoever loves perfectly keeps the Law perfectly. Whoever keeps the Law perfectly reigns supreme over the Law; Law no longer reigns supreme over him. Law is swallowed up by love. The book of James defines love as the royal Law. "If you really fulfill the royal law, according to the scripture, 'You shall love your neighbor as yourself,' you do well." [1] But as we said, everyone knows that we do not perfectly carry out the love of God incarnate in us as His image, for we can never be God. We violate the Law. And if we fail to keep one part of it, for instance:

>   mercy
>   compassion
>   patience
>   kindness
>   forgiveness
>   and so on,

we have missed the mark. We haven't measured up to perfect love, the image within us. We have broken our relationship with God.

This human weakness motivated both Job and Samuel to yearn for a mediator:

> "God is not a mortal like me, so I cannot argue
> with him or take him to trial. If only there were
> a mediator who could bring us together. . ."
> Job 9:32, 33, NLT

> "If someone sins against another person, God
> can mediate for the guilty party. But if someone
> sins against the Lord, who can intercede?"
> 1 Samuel 2:25, NLT

Great religions and philosophies throughout the ages have understood this same need for a mediator, because to them life consists of trying to "do good, do good, do good," a standard no one can attain. Because of man's sin, Law cannot mediate. All it can do is judge and condemn. If God's glory is to be restored in people's hearts, and if people are to find acceptance before God, they need a better mediator than the Law. The Law's judgment has already been made, and it is condemnation: As you sow, so shall you reap.

**If people are to find acceptance before God,
they need a better mediator than the Law.**

However, though Law cannot mediate, it is inherently designed to bring us to the mediator.

Who Can Mediate?

So who can mediate for us? Who can bridge the gap between us and God? Only Someone who, by loving perfectly, can obey the Law God has given us.

When we speak of love as being the only power that can

accomplish all that the Law demands, there should be no mistake as to how supreme that love truly is. What is the nature of such love? We can identify it within our hearts.

1. <u>Love comes from a heart that is genuine.</u>
   > "Love is patient, love is kind, and is not jealous; love does not brag and is not arrogant, does not act unbecomingly; it does not seek its own, is not provoked, does not take into account a wrong suffered, does not rejoice in unrighteousness, but rejoices with the truth; bears all things, believes all things, hopes all things, endures all things. Love never fails."
   >
   > 1 Corinthians 13:4-8

   These attributes are some of the criteria by which we know love. They are qualities of eternity. A world where love and only love reigns supreme would produce abundant life. Sin would no longer have dominion. We would not live under Law but under grace.

2. <u>The nature of love is to forgive.</u>

   In ancient times, the whole world saw pain and suffering as an effect of previous evil actions, the Law of karma. Asian philosophy sings the same tune, even today: "We are our karma; we came from our karma; we will be our karma. Every evil action must have its effect upon the person's future." There is no forgiveness, no second chance with Law. Consequences are inevitable. But perfect love forgives. And only God can love perfectly.

3. <u>Love is active and creative.</u>

   Two of the greatest facts we know are:
   [1] at the very center of our beings is life,

[2] at the very center of ultimate happiness is pure love. Love's very nature is to give life. Love must express itself; it must interact. For example, if a boy loves a girl, he is consumed by the desire to have her see and feel and receive his love. Love is not static, but always seeks new ways to communicate itself.

God's love is the eternal Now,
> constantly new and creative, yet never changing,
>> eternal and eternally faithful,
>>> yet always in a state of "becoming,"
>>>> always creating its beauty and glory in creation,
>>>>> expressing itself to its beloved humanity,
>>>>>> and recreating Himself in us.

Divine love keeps the whole material world moving; it is the creative energy that scientists seek to discover and define. It acts as the highest expression of unselfishness.

4. <u>Vicarious giving of self is the highest expression of love</u>.

"Greater love has no one than this, that he lay down his life" so that others, too, might have life and love. [2] Everyone knows this. Self-sacrificial love is the supreme concept that
> fulfills
>> redeems
>>> exonerates
>>>> glorifies
>>>>> crowns
>>>>>> all of creation.

The human heart yearns for love that is genuine, forgiving, active, creative, and self-sacrificial. This kind of love would fulfill Law and exemplify perfect karma. But human action cannot perfectly love like this.

Only God's love is perfectly genuine, forgiving, active, creative, and self-sacrificial. Then why won't the world allow God to love as we know we ought to love? Why won't the world allow God to fulfill the Law as we know we ought to fulfill the Law? Why won't the world allow God to forgive sins as we know we ought to forgive others of their sins against us?

The truth is, God Himself is willing to do everything that He requires of us. In fact, everything God's love requires of us, God *has done* Himself. But how could He, unless He were human?

By incarnating His image within us, God has given us the knowledge that He Himself can be incarnated in human form. This should not seem strange. We know that we ourselves are incarnate. God has put life and love and personality into our bodies. This is a knowing that we know. So it is rational to think that God could become man.

God Himself is willing to do everything that He requires of us.

Besides, God always intended for His *love* to mediate. He never said we would be justified by keeping the Law. He never meant for Law to be our mediator. He knows that only He can fulfill His own image incarnated within us. We can never live up to this image of divine love, even if we could reincarnate through six million lifetimes. So it is an absolute necessity for God to do what we cannot do: live up to His own image of love in us by keeping the Law. God must come in the flesh to fulfill His own human requirements. The Law was made for humans, even though God is the only one who can keep it. Therefore, if the Law

is to be kept perfectly,
> God must become like us,
>> Born of a woman,
>>> Born under the Law,
>>>> To do for man
>>>>> What he cannot do for himself.

Only God appearing in the form of man can manifest His true heart and character as perfect divine love that fulfills the universal Law written on all hearts. This is exactly what God performed when He incarnated Himself in Jesus Christ. In Jesus, God's love was incarnate.

> "But when the fullness of time had come,
> God sent his Son, born of a woman, born under the law,
> in order to redeem those who were under the law,
> so that we might receive adoption as children.
> And because you are children,
> God has sent the Spirit of his Son into our hearts,
> crying 'Abba! Father!'"
> Galatians 4:4-6, NRSV

Jesus, God's Love Incarnate

Jesus came proclaiming not only that God is good and loves the world, but also that He Himself came to fulfill the Law. That would be an absurd statement for a human being to make. Yet He said, "The Father has sent me," and "If you see me, you see the Father." [3]

If God came into the world as a man, would He not live and act as God among humans? Since love is humble and unselfish, He would be humble and unselfish, coming as a servant and fulfilling the Law by His perfect love. When Love dips down in His divine presence, free of any shackles of sin and selfishness, He expresses Himself and declares Himself by freeing suffering humanity from the bondage of the Law.

Is this what happened? In the gospels, we have a selected portion of Christ's life and teachings. These accounts all bear witness to God's incarnation. For if God became one of us, He would:
  receive the children
    reach to outsiders
      touch the lepers, heal the sick
        raise the dead
          explain His ways of love:
            "Come to me, you who are weary."
            "God loves the world."
              "If you hate your brother, you're a murderer."
                "The only way you can know God's reign in your life is to be poor in spirit. . .Blessed are the pure in heart, for they shall see God. . ."
                  "You will be perfect, even as my Father is perfect."

We know in our hearts that if and when God came, He would *have* to express His love in these ways. What's more, God, being perfect love, would have to do what the whole world believed could not be done: forgive sins.

Jesus' disciples once saw a man who had been born blind. They asked, "Who sinned: this man or his parents?" Jesus answered that neither had sinned. Then He healed the blind man. This miracle spoke volumes to those who believed that the man was blind because of his sins, his bad karma. His healing was equivalent to saying his sins had been forgiven, his bad karma erased. This amazed the people.

On another occasion, a paralyzed man was brought to Jesus. Jesus did not say, "Pick up your bed and walk." Instead, he said, "Your sins are forgiven." This was new. Never before had anyone come forgiving sins. [4]

The rulers took offense and challenged him. "Only God can forgive sins."

Jesus replied, "Which is easier to say: 'Your sins are forgiven,' or 'Take up your bed and walk'?" Jesus was pointing out their bad theology, their belief that sins could not be forgiven, their karma could not be erased. [5]

In Jesus, the world at last saw a worthy mediator, One who perfectly exemplified genuine, forgiving, active, creative, self-sacrificial love. It takes a man to mediate for man and God to mediate for God. By perfect love, the God-man became the mediator.

The Divine Scheme

In the introduction to this book, I told about a young student who challenged me 44 years ago, asking, "What is God doing? Playing a game?" This is the answer to his question: From the beginning, by creating humanity to bear the image of His love, God foreknew and predestined that mankind could not actually do what He had created them to do. So what happens in this world is ultimately God's problem. He is the Creator. He has placed the knowledge of goodness, the Law of nature within us. If the Law's goodness and justice are death to us rather than life, God is the one who made it too difficult. The imperfection, of course, lies with us, not with God or His Law. Still, God must do something about this Law, which is perfect, but impossible to keep.

God took on this responsibility when He created us. His plan was for mankind to have the very life of God, as well as the knowledge of both good and evil. Aware that man could not love as He did, God knew that eventually He Himself would have to redeem mankind from the Law that would bring sin, death, and condemnation.

It is interesting to note that stories, myths, and legends that have been enjoyed for thousands of years, as well as more recent stories such as <u>Star Wars</u> and <u>The Matrix</u>, always have a redeemer, a hero who embodies love, courage, justice, and righteousness. The story hero slays the evil one who brings misery and death. It is only right that in all cultures we should expect to see myths and legends that express the victory of love and life over evil and death. The fact is, this is exactly what we find, for these *stories and myths are rooted in what we know we know*. Mankind longs for grace to overcome Law, the hero to overcome evil and death. But no human can ultimately succeed as the hero over Law and evil and death. God Himself had to become our Divine Hero and complete His own work of life in His created beings. God Himself had to fulfill the Law for us and slay the power of sin and the sting of death. C.S. Lewis wrote:

> If ever a myth had become fact, had been incarnated, it would be just like this [the story of Jesus]. And nothing else in literature was just like this. Myths were like it in one way. Histories were like it in another. But nothing was simply like it. And no person was like the Person it depicted....Here and here only in all time the myth must have become fact; the Word, flesh; God, Man. [6] (parentheses mine)

In Jesus, the Divine Hero became a son of man to do the work of *life*. He *lived* perfectly on our behalf, as One who kept the Law. But life and death are not separate entities. Death is part of life, even though the only reason the body dies is because sin curses both man's physical body as well as his spirit. And what about the sin of the world? The karma must be worked out. So Jesus also *died* perfectly on our behalf, as One who kept the Law.

In Jesus, God gave His life on the cross that we might live. "I lay down my life," He said. "No one takes it from me, but I lay it down of my own accord." ⁷ Through Jesus' life and death, God Himself fulfilled the Law with perfect justice and perfect mercy. ⁸ God defused the arguments of religions and philosophies that were saying, "God should keep the Law." ⁹ But no one expected that God truly would keep the Law as man.

Yet it was not Jesus' death that completed the work. It was Jesus' resurrection from the grave that established the victory over sin and death, proving that the tomb of death could not hold the Life of God. Being raised by the Spirit, Jesus took away the sin of the world so that grace could reign over Law.

But God's redeeming grace was not only for sin. Jesus' physical resurrection demonstrated that God's grace also applied to the curse of death on our bodies. Although man is first created as a physical body, his only hope is in a spiritual body. Jesus' resurrection swallowed death and brought us the hope of life beyond the tomb.

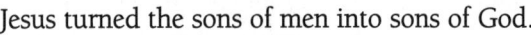

Jesus turned the sons of men into sons of God.

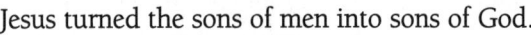

C.S. Lewis finds the work of a diver a fitting analogy for God's work of redemption:

> One has a picture. . . .of a diver, stripping off garment after garment, making himself naked, then flashing for a moment in the air, and then down through the green, and warm, and sunlit water into the pitch-black, cold, freezing water, down into the mud and slime, then up again, his lungs almost bursting, back again to the green and warm and sunlit water, and then at

last out into the sunshine, holding in his hand the dripping thing he went down to get. This thing is human nature; but, associated with it, all Nature, the new universe. [10]

Jesus as God-man did what the Law could never do: mediate between man and God. The Divine Hero, revealed as Jesus the Son of God, became a son of man and by His karma of perfect obedience made us righteous. Jesus turned the sons of men into sons of God. The apostle Paul said it this way:

> Jesus "is the image of the invisible God, the first-born of all creation. For by Him all things were created, both in the heavens and on earth, visible and invisible, whether thrones or dominions or rulers or authorities — all things have been created by Him and for Him. And He is before all things, and in Him all things hold together. He is also the head of the body, the church; and He is the beginning, the first-born from the dead; so that He Himself might come to have first place in everything. For it was the Father's good pleasure for all the fullness to dwell in Him, and through Him to reconcile all things to Himself, having made peace through the blood of His cross; through Him, I say, whether things on earth or things in heaven. And although you were formerly alienated and hostile in mind, engaged in evil deeds, yet He has now reconciled you in His fleshly body through death, in order to present you before Him holy and blameless and beyond reproach."
>
> Colossians 1:15-22

God in Jesus Christ, kept the Law perfectly, fulfilling Law by His love and grace. Love and grace do not dispense with Law, but become the elements by which Law is fulfilled. Thus love and grace become the ruling factors, and Jesus Christ reigns supreme over the Law. *Now, though Law sets the standard within all men, it is love that reigns over all men through Jesus.* For when He extends forgiveness and grace by His love, the karmic effect of Law on sin is annulled. Total redemption has taken place righteously and justly in the eyes of God.

If we embrace that redemption, then the life of sin and death is the true illusion, the dimension of what is passing. We are not of the world, but have been translated out of the power of darkness into the kingdom of God. Righteousness reigns over us. We walk in the light. We have escaped.

Total redemption has taken place in the eyes of God.
Righteousness reigns over us.
We have escaped.

Summary: Chapter 7

Man knows he needs a mediator.
Law cannot mediate; it can only condemn.
But Law is designed to bring us to the mediator.
Only perfect love can fulfill the Law.
Love is genuine, forgiving, active, creative, and self-giving.
Only God is perfectly loving: genuine, forgiving, active, creative, self-giving.
God always intended for His love to mediate.
Since we are incarnate beings, it is reasonable to think that God can incarnate Himself.
Jesus came to do the work of life.
Jesus came to do the work of death.
Jesus' resurrection established victory over sin and death.
Law sets the standard, but now love reigns over Law.
God kept the Law for us by becoming a man.

1 James 2:8

2 John 15:13

3 John 14:9, 24

4 John 9:1-12

5 Matthew 9:2-8

6 C. S. Lewis, Surprised by Joy (A Harvest Book, Harcourt, 1955, San Diego, New York, London) 236.

7 John 10:17, 18, RSV

8 Man under Law failed in one point and as a result must receive the consequence of his evil karma. That point has been recorded in Genesis 3, as the fall of man. From the resultant physical and spiritual death the saying arises, "the wages of sin is death." Death is separation. To die spiritually is to be separated from God by sin. So for men under Law, two things are inevitable:
    1. Man will always sin and thus be separated from God.
       Man will never have oneness with God as long as sin is there.
    2. The Law can never be fulfilled by sinful man. Law can never be destroyed, only fulfilled.
The requirement that God has imposed upon Himself by creating man is that only He can keep the perfect Law, and He must do it as a man. Sin is against God, so only God has the right to forgive it and to cleanse it. Therefore, God has chosen not to destroy the Law but to fulfill it for all mankind. In the life, death and resurrection of Jesus, we find the divine scheme of why God would create human beings as free creatures with a will and why his love can redeem man from an impossible dilemma.

9 See comments by Suzuki and Plato in chapter 5.

10 C. S. Lewis, The Grand Miracle (New York: Ballantine, 1970) 59.

Interlude

The True Story of the Tiger King and His Helmsman

Ancient Siam (Thailand)

King Sua, called the Tiger King, loved two things. One was his royal barge.[1] From its bow there rose a huge ornamental dragon's head overlaid with gold. The barge was so long, it had to be powered by scores of oarsmen. So precious was this barge, that the king had made a law: If its dragon's head was ever broken, the helmsman of the barge would have his own head cut off.

The second thing the Tiger King loved was his friend Phan Thai Norasin who happened to be the helmsman for the royal barge. The king was very proud of Phan Thai's skill and loved the challenge of maneuvering his huge barge through the narrow canals.

One day the Tiger King raced his barge through the canals, around the bends, all the while asking Phan Thai to go faster and faster. In spite of Phan Thai's skill, the barge sped along too fast to make one of the curves. The dragon's head struck the limb of an overhanging tree and broke off.

The King was immediately grieved. "Never mind, Phan Thai," he said. "It was not your fault. No one could have made that turn at the speed we were going. The accident was unavoidable."

Now Phan Thai Norasin loved King Sua and was deeply loyal to him. He knew that if the king set aside the law, the people would think their ruler was showing partiality. They would accuse King Sua of abusing his authority by deciding which laws he would follow and which he would ignore. So Phan Thai said, "No, my King. I have broken the law, and the penalty is death. You must follow the law and execute me."

Still the king said, "No, it was not your fault. I made the barge go too fast for the turns."

But Phan Thai insisted. "As a king, if you do not keep the law, you belittle the law and prove yourself to be partial. You would be breaking the law yourself. That could undermine your authority as king."

The Tiger King anxiously pondered this dilemma. At last, he had an idea. He had a statue made of Phan Thai Norasin. Then he had the executioner cut off the head of the statue. "There!" he said. "The law has been fulfilled."

"No," said Phan Thai. "The law has not been fulfilled. The statue is not me. It was I who broke the law." He continued to insist that he must be executed to fulfill the law's just demands.

The king agonized over the decision he had to make. He himself had commanded the royal barge to go faster. Now he felt responsible. But the law was the law. It could not mediate for the violator. It could only punish. As history tells it, the Tiger King finally executed his dear friend Phan Thai Norasin.

This story, taught to school children throughout Thailand, can provide an analogy for us, showing that people need to find forgiveness and mercy, but cannot find it in Law. King Sua saw the need in this instance, and agonizingly looked for a way around the requirement of the law. But a statue which looked like Phan Thai Norasin could not mediate, and mercy could not be extended. Even the king could not set aside the law.

---

[1] The royal barge is still used by the King of Thailand on special occasions. Even today, it can be seen in Bangkok.

CHAPTER EIGHT

From Sons of Men to Sons of God

"For there is one God and one Mediator between God and men, the Man Christ Jesus."
1 Timothy 2:5, NKJV

"For God has done what the law, . . .could not do: sending his own son in the likeness of sinful flesh and for sin, . . .in order that the just requirement of the law might be fulfilled in us, who walk not according to the flesh but according to the Spirit."
Romans 8:3, 4

A Solution for the Tiger King

The story of Phan Thai Norasin and the Tiger King ends tragically with the inability of even the King himself to save his friend Phan Thai from execution under an immutable law. But suppose we found King Sua upon his bed in the heat of the tropical sun, mulling over his troubles: "The problem is great, for the demand of the law must be fulfilled. If I do not execute Phan Thai, the people will say that I am partial. They will say that I believe a ruler can do whatever he wants and does not have to follow the law. But I do not want Phan Thai to die. How can I do justice to the law, yet have mercy on Phan Thai?"

As the king ponders, he comes upon a solution. "Tomorrow I shall announce to the people that I bear a direct responsibility for this. I required Phan Thai to guide the boat too fast. No one could have done it successfully. So I shall be executed in Phan Thai's place, and the just requirements of the law will be met. Also, I shall decree a new law. From this day forward, the king will be able to give grace and mercy in administering the law."

In this way, King Sua could have fulfilled the law and saved a friend while honoring the kingship. But in reality, the royalty of Siam were untouchable, and the king's death on behalf of a friend would have been an impossible idea. So, although the law was holy in its intent, just in its demands, and good in its accomplishments, it provided no mercy to the violator. A Law intended to be good had become a Law of sin and death. The Law was inexorable and immutable. Even the king had to obey it.

A Law intended to be good had become a Law of sin and death.

Just to illustrate a point, suppose we insert Phan Thai Norasin for "us" and King Sua for "Jesus Christ" in Romans 5:

> For while Phan Thai Norasin was still helpless, at the right time King Sua died for Phan Thai. For one will hardly die for a righteous man, though perhaps for the good man someone would dare even to die. But King Sua demonstrates his own love toward Phan Thai Norasin, in that while Phan Thai was yet a sinner, King Sua died for him. Much more then, having now been justified by the king's

blood, Phan Thai Norasin shall be saved from
the wrath of the law through the king's death.

The analogy is not perfect, because King Sua, unlike Christ, was not perfect, and Phan Thai represents one man instead of all humanity. But this illustration does help us to understand the problem of the Law of karma (human action) and the need it creates for God to act if man is to be redeemed from a sinful, suffering world. In this case, the only justifiable, lawful way out of the dilemma of executing Phan Thai Norasin would be for the king himself to fulfill the law by dying in Phan Thai's place. We, like Phan Thai, are all violators of the Law. He was a violator of law before King Sua, and we are all sinners before God.

The Transfer of Karma

As we have seen, God is not angry or wrathful about our sins. But according to Law, the effects of our sin must be reaped. So God incarnated Himself in Jesus to do for man what man could not do for himself: fulfill the Law. Yet just as God allows us free choice, He also allowed Jesus to choose: "Back off, or stand firm." Jesus could have run away from death. In fact, He asked the Father, "Let this cup pass from me." But God allowed the karma of those who hated Jesus to play itself out. In the end, Jesus chose to drink the cup of bitterness, the sin of humanity. His mission was: "I came to fulfill the Law."

The crucifixion of Jesus Christ was not an act of God. *It was not God who killed Jesus.* The crucifixion was an inhumanity in which God willfully refused to interfere. As God-man, Jesus could have called tens of thousands of angels to save Himself. But God has never exerted carnal authority over the free will of man. He lets the Law of cause and effect take its course. So the crucifixion of Christ was an act freely and willfully done by men who hated His lifestyle of loving all equally,

> Jew and Gentile,
>> saint and sinner,
>>> male and female,
>>>> slave and master.

Those who opposed Jesus resented His proclamation that God so loved the world that He gave His only Son so that people would not have to reap their karma. They could not perceive the incarnation of God as flesh and blood.

So Jesus reaped what humanity had sown. His message was, "I will take your sin upon me and receive the consequence. I will pay the ransom. You can receive my life, if you will accept my death."

The Mystery of Freedom

The mystery that remains is: How can the karma of One who fulfills the Law (Jesus) be transferred to those who have broken the Law? There are two sides to the answer: God's side and man's side.

From God's side, there are only two solutions:
1. Destroy the Law. This would result in chaos and a hopeless universe.
2. Fulfill the Law. This would keep the promise of life that Law offers.

While there are many people, there is only one Law. God does not have to fulfill the Law for one person at a time. He only has to fulfill the Law once and for all.[1] Once the Law is fulfilled, love becomes the reigning factor over *all* humanity.

From man's side, think of parent and child. How can the forgiveness of a father be transferred to a son who has sinned terribly against him? The transfer is made by the son's belief and acceptance of his father's forgiveness. If we see God as the parent and humanity as the son, then we see that the combined karma (action) of all human beings is sin (singular). So the one God-man fulfills the one Law for the sin of humanity. But God has given each individual free will. Each person is free to make his own choices and experience the effects of his own karma. So although God Himself fulfilled the Law once for all through Christ Jesus, each person is free to accept or reject that gift of grace.

If we reject grace, the Law still has power over us as lawbreakers, for the Law of karma must be fulfilled. But if we accept grace, the Law operates on Jesus' karma, and we are set free from the Law of sin and death. (We will see this more clearly in chapter 11.)

So there is *One* God. There is *one* Law. The world, His creation, is a whole, one entity bearing the sin of *one* humanity. When the One God, becoming human, fulfills the one Law for His one creation, His karma is transferred to all who will accept it.

Now see how Paul addresses this very issue:

> . . . sin entered the world through one man, and death through sin, and in this way death came to all men, because all sinned . . . . For if, by the trespass of the one man, death reigned through that one man, how much more will those who receive God's abundant provision of grace and of the gift of righteousness reign in life through the one man, Jesus Christ.
> Romans 5:12, 17, NIV

And:

> For all have sinned and fall short of the glory of God, and are justified freely by his grace through the redemption that came by Christ Jesus. God presented him as a sacrifice of atonement, through faith in his blood. He did this to demonstrate his justice, because in his forbearance he had left the sins committed beforehand unpunished —he did it to demonstrate his justice at the present time, so as to be just and the one who justifies those who have faith in Jesus.
> Romans 3:23-26, NIV

God's whole purpose was to take away sin and the concept of wrath, which Law created, by fulfilling the Law and replacing it with love. But justice demands that the old Law be accomplished. The wages of sin was death. Therefore, Jesus had to die.

Self-Verifying Truth

When we see Jesus, His life, His death, and His resurrection, He corresponds to what we know we know: God is perfect love. Only perfect love can fulfill the Law. So only God can fulfill the Law. But the Law is for man. So only God *as man* can fulfill the Law. This He did.

To see how this Truth verifies itself, join me in a Truth-seeking dialogue, typical of the many conversations I have had around the world from university campuses to simple bamboo huts. All these dialogues have taken a similar path as in the following discussion between Phan, a young Thai man, and me, whom the Thais call "Ahjan," or teacher.

Phan and I sit cross-legged on a teakwood floor, on opposite sides of a low, round rattan table on which is a snack of sticky rice and spicy dipping sauce. Even though this is a deep and life-determining discussion, there is still a twinkle of humor between us, and we are both smiling as we work through this together. In our discussion, we have just come to the pinnacle of the dilemma of the law. Listen to how the Truth flows naturally in Phan's answers, coming not from what he's learned, but from what he already knows in the depths of his heart. Hear how Truth is self-verifying.

Ahjan: Did you create the world?
Phan: No.
Ahjan: Are you sure?
Phan: Yes.
Ahjan: How can you be sure?
Phan: Because I am just human, not God.

Ahjan: Can you be perfect love and goodness as God is perfect love and goodness?
Phan: No.
Ahjan: Why can you not love perfectly as God loves?
Phan: I am not God.
Ahjan: Ah. So the creation can never be the Creator. The Law of love that God has given (be kind, have mercy, forgive, be true), is this to give life or to destroy life?
Phan: To give life.
Ahjan: If you do good, you get what?
Phan: You get good, because of the Law of karma.
Ahjan: So are you saying the cause and effect principle of the Law must be fulfilled?
Phan: Yes, there is no other way.
Ahjan: We've established that love fulfills the whole Law. Are the attributes of love commands for animals — fish, birds, dogs?
Phan: No, they are for people.
Ahjan: Is the Law given for people to keep or for God?
Phan: For people.
Ahjan: This Law is holy and just and good. Is it for life or death?
Phan: For life.
Ahjan: It's for life, but it brings death. Why?
Phan: Because people cannot keep it.
Ahjan: So you agree that people cannot keep the Law perfectly. Do you know this, or must it be proved?
Phan: I know it. But the Law must be satisfied. That is, if you do good, you get good; if you do evil, you get evil. Everybody knows that karma must work itself out.
Ahjan: Is there any escape from the law of karma?
Phan: No.
Ahjan: So the Law was given for people. People cannot do it. The Law

Phan: is unchangeable and must be satisfied.

Phan: It doesn't sound honorable to say that God created man, yet knew from the beginning that man could not keep the Law. It sounds like God is playing games with us.

Ahjan: It's true that God knew man could not keep the Law. But He also knew that the same love, holiness, justice, and goodness that embodies the whole Law can find fulfillment and completeness in His own love. He knew the creation could not keep the Law and that He would have to provide a way out for mankind. If man cannot keep the Law, who is the only one who can keep it?

Phan: God.

Ahjan: God is the only one who can keep the Law. Yet it was made for man. Therefore, if the Law is to be kept perfectly,

> God must become like us,
>> Born of a woman,
>>> Born under the Law,
>>>> To do for man
>>>>> What he cannot do for himself
>>>>>> In order that the sons of men [2]
>>>>>>> Can become sons of God.

∽

**The Truth verifies itself.
It's just that way.**

∽

Summary: Chapter 8

We all violate the Law.
God allowed Jesus to choose whether to die or not.
The crucifixion of Jesus was not an act of God.
God allowed the destructive karma of men to work itself out.
Jesus reaped what humanity had sown.
God had to either destroy the Law or fulfill it.
When One God, becoming human, fulfills the one Law for His one creation, His karma is transferred to all who will accept it.
Truth is self-verifying.
If the Law is to be kept perfectly,
>God must become man,
>>born of a woman,
>>>born under the Law.
>>>>to do for man
>>>>>what he cannot do for himself
>>>>>>in order that the sons of men
>>>>>>>can become sons of God.

[1] Romans 5:12, 15, 18-20

[2] We are called "sons of men" because we are the creation. "Sons of men" cannot keep the Law perfectly. They inherit their nature from the first man.

CHAPTER NINE

Christ Unrealized and Christ Realized

"Thou art the Christ, the Son of the living God."
Matthew 16:16

Who is the Christ?

The word "Christ" comes from a Greek word which literally means "the anointed one." "Christos" (Christ) is the Greek translation of the Hebrew word "messiah," from Hebrew "mashiah," "anointed one." Before Jesus came, the term "messiah" was not a proper noun but a descriptive, a common noun, a generic word. "Messiah" or "christ" was a term applied to various people who were "anointed" or "sent by God." In the political sphere, the word referred to kings who continued the rule of David. In a religious sense, it applied to priests or others divinely appointed for a certain task among the chosen people. In prophetic expectation, it referred to an ideal Davidic king raised up by God and placed on the throne of Israel. Isaiah used the term "messiah," "anointed," to describe Cyrus as God's agent in the affairs of His people.

When the book of Matthew was translated into Greek, "messiah" was translated "christos," or in the English version "christ." The Greeks, like the Hebrews, applied this term to rulers or priests.

Christ In Every Man

Today, most Christians see "messiah" or "christ" as only a Judeo-

Christian concept, because Christians know that Jesus is the Christ. So we assume that the definition of "christ" has always been Jesus. But that is not so. It is important to realize that it was not only the Jews who looked for a messiah. Even before Jesus came, there was the concept of a mediator in many cultures, although the term was not understood in the same way the Jews culturally understood the term. Still, various animistic, primitive religions have mythologies of some type that look for a mediator.

For example, the Karen (Kah-rin') tribes of Burma and northern Thailand and the Lahu (Lah'-hoo) of southeast Asia and southern China had legends of the coming of the "man in white," or "the man with the white book," or "the man on a white horse coming as a redeemer for their peoples." [1] In British tradition until the 19th or 20th century, each village had a "sin-eater." This person would go to the bedsides of those who were dying. A bit of bread would be placed on the dying person's chest, and the sin-eater would pray. Then the sin-eater would eat the bit of bread to signify that the dying person's sin had been removed and taken into the sin-eater. [2]

> Even before Jesus came,
> there was the concept of a mediator in many cultures.

Many of today's popular philosophies also acknowledge the concept of a "christ." I discovered this in 1995 as I was headed home on furlough from Asia. I was sitting in the John Wayne airport in Long Beach, California, waiting through a three-hour layover. Next to me sat a man who had a laptop computer. Having been in Asia for several years, I had not seen many laptops, so I asked him about it. In the course of the conversation, we introduced ourselves to each other. He told me that he was the son of a prominent leader of the New Age movement in Dallas, Texas. As we talked about religion, he made a statement that I had never heard anyone say before. He said, "Christ is in every man."

When the young man made this statement, he was affirming a belief in "christ-consciousness." He was affirming the necessity of forgiveness, grace, and righteousness. He was affirming the image of God in every person. He was not, however, sanctioning the deity of Jesus or acknowledging Jesus as the Christ. *Christ* is a neutral word. *Jesus* is not. When we speak of Jesus as the Christ, the word *Christ* then becomes a personal, proper noun.

Christ was not put within us by our believing in Jesus. Instead, the christ within us found fulfillment only in Jesus.

When the gospel is presented, all people hear the Truth, which corresponds to God's image within them. However, Paul found that the minds of unbelievers had been blinded by the "god of this world" so that they could not be enlightened about Christ, "who is the image of God." But for those who believe, God has enlightened their hearts to show who He is in Jesus.

So as Christians, we realize that Jesus is the Christ within us. But christ was not put there by our believing in Jesus. Instead, the christ within us found fulfillment only in Jesus. We turn and witness this same Jesus to someone else so that they, too, may experience the fulfillment of the Truth within them. Because:

Every person is created in the image of God.
   Christ is the image of God.
      Therefore, the image of God within us is Christ.
         "Christ in you, the hope of glory."
            Christ in every man, the hope of glory. [3]

The "Aha" Moment

> (Jesus) said to them, "But who do you say that I am?" And Simon Peter answered and said, "Thou art the Christ, the Son of the living God." And Jesus answered and said to him, "Blessed are you, Simon Barjona, because flesh and blood did not reveal this to you, but My Father who is in heaven."
>
> Matthew 16:15-17

Peter's confession, "You are the Christ," showed his recognition of Jesus as the Messiah. Peter's realization transcended the politicized concept of messiah that had become popular in that day. That concept was that a deliverer would come to free the Jews from the Romans and establish a physical Jewish kingdom. Peter saw Jesus not just as *a* messiah, *a* christ, but *the* Messiah, *the* Christ sent from God, of God, to be God with man.

Jesus Christ is the fleshly fulfillment of the unrealized christ within.

It is important to note that Peter did not base his statement on physical evidence, but on the sudden spiritual understanding that this Jesus, who stood before him, was the Anointed One, the Mediator, the Savior, the Deliverer for whom all the world was waiting. This understanding was communicated from the Spirit of God to Peter's spirit. Jesus confirmed this when he said, "Flesh and blood have not revealed this to you, but my Father. . ."

People all over the world may see Christ like Peter did, in an "Aha" moment, and then, like Peter, run from this realization, deny it, and fight against it. But God's desire is that when people hear about His ultimate act of love, His death for the sin of the world, they, too, will have an "Aha" moment and cry out, "*Jesus* is the Christ, the Son of the living God." This acknowledgement of the Christ within us is
> the image of God in every man
>> the breath of God in every man
>>> the life of God in every man
>>>> the spirit of God in every man
>>>>> the hope of glory to every man,

a hope *realized* only in Jesus Christ: a hope of release from sin, a hope for freedom from illusion, and the instant realization that with a new birth of the Spirit, the old self ceases to exist, and the new self comes into being. The Christian's deep desire must be to present this gospel so clearly that people easily recognize that Jesus Christ is the fleshly fulfillment of the unrealized christ within them.

Summary: Chapter 9

"Christ" means "the anointed one."
Historically, "christ" applied to people who were divinely appointed.
Many philosophies today acknowledge a "christ-consciousness."
Yet this christ is realized only in Jesus.
Peter realized that Jesus was *the* Christ,
> because the Spirit of God revealed it to him.

[1] Don Richardson, <u>Eternity in their Hearts</u> (Ventura, CA: Regal, 1981).

[2] "SIN-EATER, a man who for trifling payment was believed to take upon himself, by means of food and drink, the sins of a deceased person. The custom was once common in many parts of England and in the highlands of Scotland . . . . The custom of sin-eating is generally supposed to be derived from the scapegoat (q.v.) in Leviticus xvi.21, 22." "SIN-EATER" *LoveToKnow 1911 Online Encyclopedia.* copyright 2003, 2004 LoveToKnow, 16 October 2004 <http://96.1911encyclopedia.org/S/SI/SIN_EATER.htm>

[3] Genesis 1:26, 27, Colossians 1:15, 2 Corinthians 4:4, Colossians 1:27

CHAPTER TEN

Identifying Christ in the Hearts of the World

"In the beginning was the Word, and the Word was with God, and the Word was God. He was in the beginning with God. All things came into being through him, and without him not one thing came into being. What has come into being in him was life, and the life was the light of all people. The light shines in the darkness, and the darkness did not overcome it . . . The true light, which enlightens everyone, was coming into the world."
-John 1:1-5, 9, NRSV

As we have seen, all people have the same image of God within them and experience the same Law of human nature that guides their lives morally. Honorable people everywhere grope to understand good and to resist evil in response to that Law at work within them. Most of them are committed to making the world a more just, peaceful, and loving place in which to live. Out of this human spirit that mirrors God, religion emerges within communities. These religions perceive the need to express God's image in their various cultural and religious forms. Although they may not identify that perception as God's image, this concept of "christ" is alive in their hearts. They realize their need for a mediator, an anointed one, because they cannot find mercy by themselves.

> We realize our need for a mediator,
> because we cannot find mercy by ourselves.

The *Logos* is the christ in Every Person

When the apostle John wrote his gospel, the Spirit of God inspired him to identify Jesus as the image of God within mankind by calling Him "the light that enlightens every person." John clearly understood that God's life and light necessitated some kind of expression in terms of each person's culture. So in addressing the Greco-Roman world, he used the Greek philosophical word *Logos*.

> In the beginning was the *Logos*, and the *Logos* was with God and the *Logos* was God.... In him was life, and the life was the light of all people ... the true light that enlightens everyone. [1]

Logos was a concept that John's readers understood easily, and it came closest to identifying for them the Christ whom Jesus embodied. For the Greeks and Romans, the idea of the *Logos* bridged the chasm between mankind and the Creator. Though conceived as impersonal, the concept of the *Logos* was that it was

> an intellectual tool enabling them to express God's mysterious essence
> > the revealer of what is hidden
> > > the guide and agent of knowledge
> > > > the way of teaching righteousness and goodness
> > > > > a cosmic and creative potency.

To the Stoic philosophers, the world was a grand unfolding of the *Logos*, the power that extends throughout matter. They even equated the *Logos* "with the concept of God.... It is the principle which creates the world, i.e., which orders and constitutes it." 2

The word *Logos* had a mystery about it that the Greek and Roman philosophers could not fathom, the great Unknown about God. How could God have a relationship with a sinful, wicked world? How could mere finite man reach into the infinite immeasurable essence of God's righteousness? The Greek and Roman philosophers reasoned correctly: We can never know all there is to know about God.

But John demonstrated to the Greco-Roman world that the *Logos* is the Christ, the life and light that enlightens every person who enters the world. When fully realized, this *Logos* is "full of grace and truth." 3 It manifests the unchanging reality of God. John believed that once the Greco-Roman world understood this, they would identify Jesus Christ with their concept of the *Logos*. In the life of Jesus, understood by the Greeks as the *Logos*, the Christ, the demands of the law were satisfied. In Jesus, the mystery that haunted the Greco-Roman philosophers was solved. Could there be a mediator between man and God? John connected the *Logos* with the common denominator of Truth verified in their hearts: Christ.

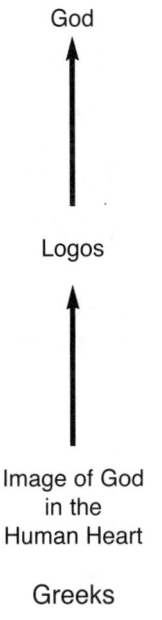

**The Logos, the Christ,
manifests the unchanging reality of God.**

The Greco-Roman "christ-consciousness" was the Logos. Can we identify a Logos-type of "christ-consciousness" in other cultures?

The Torah and the Christ

For the Jews, that which mediated the will of God for them was the Torah, or their "instruction." In their view, God was personal and had made covenant with them, but He was unapproachable, having spoken to them through the Torah, the law. When Moses made his final addresses to the people of Israel concerning the importance of the law, he told them that it was in their hearts and in their mouths so that they could do it and know it.

"For this commandment [or law] which I command you today is not too difficult for you, nor is it out of reach. It is not in heaven, that you should say, "Who will go up to heaven for us to get it for us and make us hear it, that we may observe it?" Nor is it beyond the sea, that you should say, "Who will cross the sea for us to get it for us and make us hear it, that we may observe it?" But the word is very near you, in your mouth and in your heart, that you may observe it."

- Moses in Deuteronomy 30:11-14

In his letters to the churches, Paul pointed out that "Christ is the end of the law," its accomplished purpose. [4] Then Paul quoted the above passage from Moses using the word "Christ" instead of the word "law." What Moses had called *law*, Paul called *Christ*:

> For Christ is the end of the law for righteousness to everyone who believes. For Moses writes that the man who practices the righteousness which is based on the law shall live by that righteousness. But the righteousness based on faith speaks thus,

> "*Do not say in your Heart, 'Who will ascend into heaven?* (that is to bring Christ down).' Or '*Who will descend into the abyss?* (that is to bring Christ up from the dead).' But what does it say? '*The word is near you, in your mouth and in your heart*' that is, the word of faith which we are preaching.
>
> Paul in Romans 10:4-8

So according to Paul, the Torah, when completely realized in a person's heart and mind is Christ, "that you may know him and obey him."

The Dhamma and the Christ

The Bible does not deal with Buddhism directly, although Buddhism had existed since the sixth century B.C. But in Buddhism and other Eastern religions and philosophies, we can identify the concept of Christ by using the same principle that John used in denoting Christ as Logos and that Paul used in demonstrating that Christ is the end of the Torah. What the Greeks called the Logos, the Buddhists call the dhamma. Actually, Greek Stoicism and Buddhism are essentially twin sisters that arose about the same time in history, but in different parts of the world.

> Dhamma (dharma) means the universal truth proclaimed by Buddha. The Dhamma is itself ontologically anterior [predates] even to the Buddha, who is also the expression or historical manifestation of the Dhamma. . . .Buddhas appear, at intervals, in course of time; they come and go, but the Dhamma, as it were, goes on for ever. In this usage, Dhamma corresponds in some sense to the Greek concept of the *Logos*. [5]

Dhamma, like the *Logos*, is a way of teaching, a mysterious guide. When taken in and learned, it leads to enlightenment. When Buddha received his enlightenment, it was the dhamma that enlightened him.

> Dhamma is, literally, 'that which supports'; it is the Truth within us, relying upon which and by practising which, we can cross over the ocean of troubles and worries. Dhamma is also the formulations of this Truth which we can practise if we are interestad *[sic]* to do so. [6]

Dhamma has various meanings depending on what aspect is being addressed. When referring to how something is known, the dhamma means the law of nature, which teaches about all things. In the religious sense, it is also the moral teacher, the light of right conduct. Similarly, it can mean ultimate reality or universal truth. In regard to human action, it is at times described as the law of karma, or sowing and reaping. If the discussion centers on how to get to Nirvana, the highest level a person can reach, completely void of all earthly things, then the dhamma is the raft that takes a person there. But as a raft, it is a means to an end, not an end in itself.

The dhamma teaches about the need to exercise grace and forgiveness toward others. It points to right action and escape from the world of suffering and desire; it enlightens a person about righteous conduct and good action and points to an ultimate end to be attained. The dhamma of Buddhist teaching proves itself a worthy translation or counterpart for the Logos. In fact, the Bible translation of Sri Lanka, a strongly Buddhist country,

Nirvana
↑
|
|
Dharma
↑
|
|
Image of God in the Human Heart

Buddhists

uses the dhamma in John chapter 1 to mean the Word, the Logos.

> In the beginning was the dhamma, and the dhamma was with God and the dhamma was God. . . .

The Brahman and the Christ

In Hinduism, too, God is unapproachable, immeasurably removed, and cannot be defined in terms of this wicked world. Hindus define two levels of experience in the nature of reality. One of these is the absolute, acosmic, transcendental level. Reality at this level is called Supreme Brahman, which denotes a pure consciousness everywhere in the universe but remaining outside it, just as the sun pervades all life on earth yet remains outside earth's realm. Supreme Brahman is the first principle, the cause of the universe, free from limits of time, space, and causation, from which all things are derived, all are supported, and into which all finally disappear. The ultimate purpose of life is to realize this Supreme Brahman.

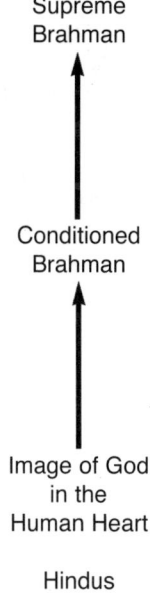

> "Verily, in the beginning this world was Brahma, the limitless One Incomprehensible is that Soul, unlimited, unborn, not to be reasoned about, unthinkable. In the dissolution of the world He alone remains awake. From that space, He, assuredly, awakes this world. . . It is thought by Him, and in Him it disappears. [7] Verily this whole world is Brahma." [8]

Yet the Hindu realizes that he has to communicate somehow with the great unapproach-able Reality. He knows that human creatures need a liberator, a mediator to whom they can pray, a personal God ready to bestow grace. So there is a second level Brahman, the conditioned Brahman, with physical attributes on the level of the relative world. Hindus can commmunicate with the conditioned Brahman. Thus, the conditioned Brahman becomes their mediator between the unapproachable Supreme Brahman and themselves. The conditioned Brahman is seen as the omnipotent and omniscient Creator, Preserver, and Destroyer of the world, and is referred to by such titles as Lord or God..

> A unique manifestation of the conditioned Brahman is the Avatar or incarnation of God, to fulfill a cosmic need whenever such a need arises. [9]

The Tao and the Christ

The concept of Tao (Way, Path, or System) has been imbedded in Chinese thought for centuries. Lao Tze (born between 570 - 604 B.C.) was the Chinese philosopher who propounded the concept of the Way (Tao) from which the religion of Taoism arose. Lao Tze identified the Tao with God:

> There exists a Being undifferentiated and complete,
> Born before Heaven and earth
> Tranquil, boundless,
> Abiding alone and changing not,
> Encircling everything with exhaustion
> Fathomless, it seems to be the Source of all things.
> But characterize it as the Tao,
> Arbitrarily forcing a name upon it,
> I call it Great." (Tao Te Ching 25:1-2)

Lao Tze himself recognized that it is difficult to pin down in concrete terms exactly what the Tao is. The Tao of the universe is

Eternal. It is seen as a cosmic energy, which brings about order and harmony in heaven and earth. "All things under heaven sprang from it (Tao) as existing (and named); that existence sprang from it [as?] nonexistent (and not named)." [10]

Literally, Tao means "way" or "road." It is also a system or method of operation. But there is something beyond that. The Tao is alluded to on two levels.

> The Tao that can be trodden is not the eternal Tao.
> The name that can be named is not the eternal name.
> Having no name, it is the Originator of heaven and earth;
> having a name, it is the Mother of all things. (Tao Te Ching, 1:1-2)
> . . .As soon as it proceeds into action, it has a name.
> When it once has that name, (men) can know to rest in it. . . .
> (Ch. 32:4)

In the struggle to name that which cannot be named, one suggestion used frequently was the "One":

> Tao begets One; one begets two;
> Two begets three; three begets all things.(Ch. 42:1)
> Therefore the Sage embraces the one. (Ch. 22:2)

Though the Tao is eternal and impersonal, by following Nature's course of harmony and perfection, one attains fullness of life by present harmony with the Tao. [11] To put it in other terms, by knowing the Way and walking in it, one reaches the eternal.

> He who attains the Tao is everlasting.
> Though his body may decay he never perishes. (16:2)

The philosophers' authority was the Truth imprinted in the heart, which they identified through dialogue.

The Tao searches for the Ultimate Reality and then for how man may be in accord with that Reality. The Tao is the way to that Reality. So here in ancient Chinese philosophy and religion is a "logos-like" word used to communicate the essence, the image in mankind that is the Christ. In fact, in John 1 in the Chinese Bible, the word *Logos* is translated *Tao*.

> In the beginning was the Tao,
> and the Tao was with God
> and Tao was God ...

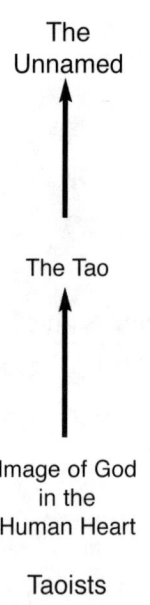

All these ancient philosophers may seem to be borrowing from one another or quoting from something else in their philosophies to prove what is truth to them. But it is not a matter of borrowing. This *is* the Truth that's written on the human heart. Greek philoso-phers, Buddha, Lao Tze, and others used dialogue to formulate their thoughts and share their teachings. Their reference material was only the human heart of the listener. In a coming chapter, we will see how Jesus Himself did this in the gospels. The authority of the appeal of these philosophers, like that of Jesus, was the Truth imprinted in the human heart by the image of God, which they identified through dialogue. This was Truth that gripped the hearts of their listeners.

The Qur'an of Islam

Because Islam takes in such a vast number of people, it's right to consider it in the search to identify "christ" in other religions. Islam came hundreds of years after Jesus Christ, and differs greatly from philosophies and religions prior to Jesus in that it is based so strongly on things that have no eternal value, such as ritual and tradition.

Islam arose about the sixth century and was influenced by already existing Jewish and Christian thought. As does Judaism and Christianity, Islam follows the same monotheistic recognition of one God whom they call Allah. Muslims recognize Jesus as a prophet of God, but not as divine. Mohammed, born around 570 A.D., established the religion of Islam. Muslims deeply revere him as the final prophet of God. Yet they themselves point out that Mohammed was nothing more than a man.

Besides worship of Allah, Islam is based on strict moral laws and cultural ritual. Islam requires obedience to the Qur'an, the sacred scriptures of Islam, which provides guidance for all areas of human life. Muslims believe the Qur'an contains the very words of God himself. (See Qur'an 85:21-22; 43:3-4; 13:39). "Whereas the divine presence for the Jew is in the law and for the Christian is in the person of (Jesus) Christ, it is in the Qur'an for the Muslim." [parentheses added] [12]

> We (God) have, without doubt,
> Send down the Message;
> And We will assuredly
> Guard it (from corruption)"   (Qur'an 15:9)

In Islam, the Qur'an serves as a roadmap for this life and the life to come. It is the primary and the final authority of all law and life. The Qur'an states:

> There has come to you
> From Allah a (new) light

> And a perspicuous Book —
> Wherewith Allah guideth all
> Who seek His good pleasure
> To ways of Peace and safety,
> And leadeth them out
> Of Darkness, by His Will,
> Unto the light — guideth them
> To a Path that is Straight. (Qur'an 5:15-16)

Because so much of the Qur'an equates ritual, ceremony, and culture with the eternal Truth of God Himself, it is inappropriate to speak of the Qur'an as being the mediator for Muslims. So the heart of the Muslim may seek after God, but the problem for the Muslim remains the same as that of the Jews and all other religions. Regardless of the belief system, people everywhere who have never heard of Jesus or do not believe in Him must approach God essentially through Law. Thus Law can prevent Muslims from having mercy and compassion on those who do not follow their rituals and forms.

Such legalism can also be found in Judaism, as well as in some denominations of Christianity. The Eastern philosophers are generally not guilty of this distortion of Truth, because they base their theology upon the natural Law and not upon ritual. However, the power of Islam is in the hearts of the people who find identity with the heart of God in varied theological expressions of Allah.

```
Allah
  ↑
  |
  |
  |
Qur'an
  ↑
  |
  |
  |
Image of God
  in the
Human Heart

Muslims
```

"Christ" Identified

As we have seen, all philosophies and religions have had some concept of a bridge to mediate across the gap that exists between themselves (the beings) and their concepts of the One we call God: the "Non-being" of the Greek philosophers, the Supreme Brahman of the Hindus, Nirvana of the Buddhists, the "Unnamed" of the Taoists. However, for all of these philosophies and religions, their concept of a mediator has essentially been Law. Even the Jews have seen Law as the mediator between themselves and God.

Fulfilling the Law is a requirement for humans. Yet it is a requirement we cannot meet, for only perfect love can live up to the Law's moral demands. So the Law cannot mediate between us and God, because it becomes the prosecutor instead of the defense lawyer. It becomes a curse to us, because we cannot keep it. We are guilty.

The image of God is in every man.
Christ is the very image of God.
Therefore, christ is in every man.

While John takes the Greek Logos and identifies it as Christ, of which Jesus is the incarnation, Paul takes the law given by Moses (the Torah) and identifies its fulfillment as Christ, the end of the Law. But Paul clearly defines that his use of the Torah does not indicate any of the rituals, ceremonies, or customs followed by the Jews. In the same way, ignoring rituals, ceremonies, and customs, we may also say that the Christ is

> the Word (Logos),
> > the dhamma,
> > > the conditioned Brahman,
> > > > the Tao,

all completely realized and brought into visual sight in the person of Jesus Christ. The love that Jesus revealed as the love of the Father for the world proves to be the fulfillment of all these concepts of the essence of Truth. As we said with the Chinese doctors, Love proves to be the essence of God that holds all things together. [13]

∼

**God's perfect Love fulfills the Law
and brings a realization of the Christ.**

∼

People have but two choices. One: like the leper, to work out by their own deeds or karma an escape from the endless cycle of cause and effect. Or two: to embrace God's fulfillment of His own Law. The Jews had the *Torah*, but the Christ who was the fulfillment of that law was as yet unrealized. To the Greek, the *Logos* was the unrealized Christ. To the Buddhist, it was the *dhamma*. To the Chinese, it was the *Tao*. God had placed this christ in them when He created them in His image. So only God would be able to bring into realization

    Christ as the Logos

        Christ as the dhamma

            Christ as the conditioned Brahman

                Christ as the Torah

                    Christ as the Tao (Way)

As long as the religions are under Law, all of these are as yet unrealized and unfulfilled. But in each case, God's perfect love fulfills the Law and brings a realization of the Christ, the same realization that inspired Peter's declaration, "*You* are the Christ, the Son of the Living God."

Identifying Christ In the Hearts of the World

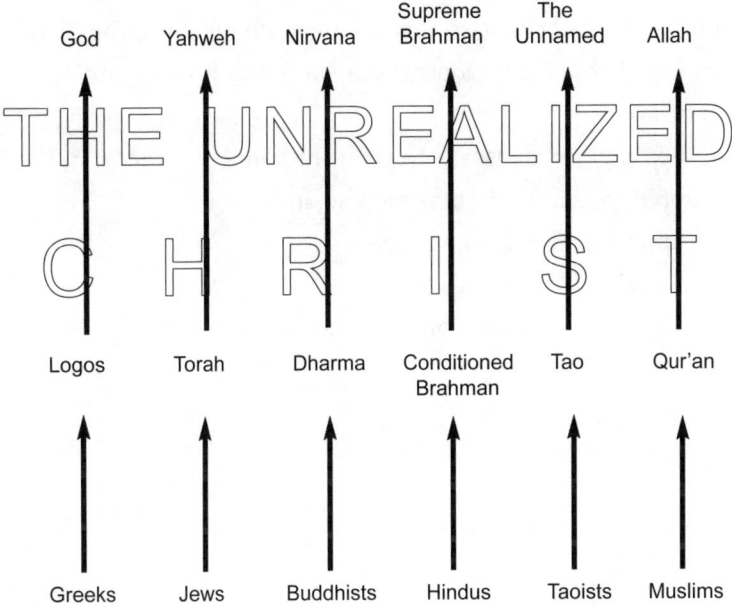

The Image of God in the Human Heart

Summary: Chapter 10

All people have the same image within them.

This is seen as the concept of a "christ-consciousness" in various cultures and religions.

John identified Jesus as this "Christ," this *Logos* or "Word," for the Greeks.

Jews knew the "Word" as the Torah.

The same concept of christ-consciousness in Buddhism is the dhamma.

The concept of christ-consciousness in Hinduism is the "conditioned Brahman."

The concept of christ-consciousness for the Chinese is the "Way" or Tao.

The approach to God in Islam is the Qur'an.

All these approach God through Law.

Only God's perfect love fulfills the Law.

God's love brings the realization that Jesus is the Christ.

1 John 1:1, 4, 9, NRSV
2 Gerhard Kittel, ed., trans. Geoffrey W. Bromley, The Theological Dictionary of the New Testament,, vol IV (Grand Rapids: Eerdmans, 1967) 84.
3 John 1:14
4 Romans 10:4
5 T.O. Ling, A Dictionary of Buddhism: A Guide to Thought and Tradition, 97.
6 Phra Khantipalo, Buddhism Explained (Bangkok: Mahamakut Rajavidyalaya, 1989) 1.
7 R. E. Hume, trans., Mait. Upanishad 6.17, The Thirteen Principle Upanishads (London: Oxford University Press, 1934), 435, as quoted in Man's Religions by John B. Noss (New York: Macmillan, 1963), 209.
8 R. E. Hume, trans., Chand. Upanishad 3.14.1, 209.
9 Swami Nikhilananda, "The Nature of Reality," Sri Ramakrishna Centre, New York, 28 November 2000 <http://www.hinduism.co.za>.

> This is a Hindu explanation of God incarnate. Because Hindu philosophy has separated a Supreme Brahman from a conditioned Brahman, thus making two gods, the conditioned Brahman has a lower state in their pantheon of gods. For this reason, the conditioned Brahman, which can be spoken of as manifesting itself as the Avatar or incarnation of God, does not represent fully the Logos of the Greeks or the dhamma of the Buddhists. But whether it's the conditioned Brahman or the Avatar, both expressions demonstrate the need for some form of mediator between man and God.

10 General references from:
   John A. Hutchison, <u>Paths of Faith</u> (New York: McGraw, 1969) 223-229.
   Direct quotes from:
   Lao Tzu, <u>Tao Te Ching</u>, trans. James Legge (Mineola, New York: Dover 1997) 21, 38, 1, 29, 39, 19, 14.

11 John B. Noss, <u>Man's Religions</u>, 3rd ed. (New York: Macmillan, 1963) 331-332, 344-350.

12 Richard Martin, ed. <u>Approaches to Islam in Religious Studies</u>, (Boston: Oneworld, 2001) 29.

13 Colossians 3:14

Interlude

Philosophies in a Nutshell

All religions and philosophies that we have looked at have a basic problem: They try to approach God through Law. If God had not written Law on our hearts, there would be much greater variety in philosophies.

Philosophy or Religion	Main Tenet or Belief
Deism	God made the world and ran away.
Greeks and Romans	God is not personal. Many gods. (Polytheism)
Hinduism	God is not personal. All is God. (Pantheism)
Buddhism and Atheism	There is no God. All is Law.
Judaism and Islam	God is personal, but He is our God, not yours.

<u>The main problem with these philosophies is</u>:

Buddhism's dhamma cannot forgive or extend mercy before the Law of cause and effect.

Hinduism's Brahman cannot forgive or extend mercy before the Law of cause and effect.

Taoism's "Unnamed" cannot forgive or extend mercy before the Law of cause and effect.

Allah of Islam gives Law that is wrathful and cannot mediate to bring forgiveness.

Judaism has a Law no one can keep.

CHAPTER ELEVEN

The Equation of Faith

"Knowing that a man is not justified by the works of the law, but by the faith of Jesus Christ, even we have believed in Jesus Christ, that we might be justified by the faith of Christ, and not by the works of the law. . . .For I through the law am dead to the law, that I might live unto God. I am crucified with Christ, nevertheless I live; yet not I, but Christ liveth in me; and the life which I now live in the flesh I live by the faith of the Son of God, who loved me, and gave himself for me."

Galatians 2:16, 19-20 KJV

We've seen that the image of God in us is Christ. The image of Christ is love. Love perfectly fulfills the law. God, incarnate in Jesus Christ, fulfilled the law for us with His perfect love. So it is not we who receive glory, but God. We now come to the last concept that will complete the transfer of glory from us back to God: faith.

The Word *Faith*

"Faith is belief," says one person.

"Faith is trust," says another.

"I was able to finish the marathon, because I had faith in myself."

"I have faith that the stock market will rally."

"Our Buick has certainly been a faithful old car."
"Your dog is such a faithful friend."
"Which faith are you?"
"I know about many of the world's faiths."
"Baptism and communion are part of the Christian faith."

Faith is hard to define, because in our current usage, we have confused the term and watered it down. We have made faith something we create by believing or not believing, doing or not doing. We have made it our creation, not God's.

**We have made faith something we create
by believing or not believing, doing or not doing.**

Sometimes we talk about faith as being personal, as being the center and core of man's knowledge, perception, and reasoning. At other times, we use the word *faith* in an impersonal way by applying it to things and animals. In that sense, it becomes a synonym for reliability or trustworthiness. People readily accept such colloquialisms, but these uses of the word obscure the true spiritual meaning. The New Testament expression, "Whatsoever is not of faith is sin" could never apply to having faith in a car or having a faithful dog.

We are also misled by expressions such as "There are many faiths," "Which faith are you?" or "You have your faith and I have mine." There are many beliefs, many guiding philosophies, many world views. Using *faith* to mean belief in this way weakens its meaning to mere opinion.

Another problem is that we make faith and belief synonymous. Even Bible dictionaries make this mistake. But if faith is belief, then faith becomes subject to man's choice: "If I don't choose to believe this, it's not my faith." However, faith is spiritual; belief is not. One's belief can be true or false, good or evil. Everything we believe is not true. What we believe may change during the course of our lifetime. Such is not the case with faith. Faith includes belief, but goes far beyond it.

Another problem is that we make faith and belief synonymous.

In addition, there is a confusion between *faith* and *trust*. Trust is a quality that enables man to rely on something or someone, but it says nothing about good and evil. Some have put their trust in the world or money, education or philosophy. Others have even put their trust in the devil. But trust in these contexts is not faith. Your dog may trust you, but your dog doesn't have faith.

Sometimes when we think of our faith, we think of the tenets and doctrines we hold. We think of our ceremonies and rituals. We say, "This is the Christian faith." Yet these cannot be faith, for there is no question that the church of the third century had significantly different rituals and ceremonies from those of the church of the first century. Western denominationalism has been divisive and sectarian for hundreds of years, each denomination with its own rituals, claiming to have the true faith. But the symbols are not our faith. (See endnote [1].)

Then What is Faith?

Because we rely on secular meanings given to the words *faith*, *belief*, and *trust*, we do not convey the spiritual message that faith is. Faith is the royal heritage of God given to enlighten all men to His heart and character revealed in Jesus Christ. Faith is the ability to find correspondence with God's heart and life. Faith is man's ability to respond to God.

Faith is the ability to find correspondence with God's heart and life.

Faith is God's gift to man. As such, it has a human factor as well as a divine factor. So we can say that the human factor of faith is:
obedience
    trust
        reliability
            constancy
                steadfastness
                    assurance
                        certainty
                            conviction.

These are the human factors of faith and are subjective. But notice that these factors are *responses* to the divine factor.

The divine factor of faith is His *substance*. "Now faith is the substance of things hoped for, the evidence of things not seen" (Hebrews 11:1, KJV). This word *substance* is the very word in which God takes out the human factor and inserts the divine. It is the same word used in Hebrews 1:3, where it is translated *person*, referring to Jesus Christ: "the brightness of his glory, and the express image of his person." So the divine factor of faith is:
the reality,
    the person,
        the nature,
            the being. . .of God.

Perhaps the simplest way to understand the meaning of the word *faith* is to think of the word *faithfulness*. The faith of Christ is actually the faithfulness of Christ. Karl Barth has pointed out that in Romans 3:24-28 the word *pistis*, Greek for *faith*, is best translated *faithfulness*. He stresses that "the law of the faithfulness of God, or what is the same thing, the law of faith, is the place where we are established by God." He translates Romans 3:27, 28 as follows:

> By what manner of law? Of works? Nay: but
> by the law of the faithfulness of God apart from
> the works of the law. [2]

So the words *faith* and *faithfulness* will be used interchangeably in the following pages.

When *faith* modifies God's action, it is always *faithfulness*. God can act no other way. But when we speak of our faith as modifying our action, our works, then we never think of faithfulness, for we are unfaithful. When we speak of being unfaithful to our faith, the first thing that comes to mind is, "I do not always obey it." Faith is the response to law that says, "I must trust it. I must obey it." *Faith enables us to approach law with the will to trust and obey.*

Hebrews 11:6 says, "Without faith, it is impossible to please Him, for he who comes to God must believe that He is, and that He is a rewarder of those who seek Him." The writer then gives an extensive list of people of old who perceived God, then walked by faith and were saved by faith. Notice how far back these people of faith go.

Abel was saved by faith.
    Noah was saved by faith.
        Abraham was saved by faith.
            Moses was saved by faith.
                Rahab the harlot was saved by faith.

Two things become evident when this list is considered. First, there was a vast dissimilarity in what all these people believed. Whatever the Hebrew writer meant when he wrote of Rahab having faith by which she was saved, he certainly did not mean the ceremonies and rituals of the Jews. Rahab probably knew nothing of circumcision or the Sabbath or the tabernacle. She knew only the conviction within her that prompted her to choose the right, and she was faithful by obeying that conviction.

Second, the Hebrew writer takes this list of people, who lived over a span of time from the very beginning down to the first century, and throws them into one common community of faith. All of them were saved by faith, he says.

So the diversity of belief and practice evident among these people is not classified as faith. They even had different beliefs about who God actually was. But whatever the writer is talking about has a common base by which each one of these people had a relationship with the living God. They were sustained throughout life and found victory by which God was glorified in those life circumstances. They were all faithful.

The indwelling Spirit of God was leading them to follow His nature, His reality, the very substance of His being.

When the Hebrew writer says "by faith," what he literally means is "by christ," yet unrealized, for he goes ahead and explains: Moses, "esteeming the reproach of Christ greater riches than the treasures of Egypt. . . . endured, as seeing him who is invisible." ³ The Hebrew writer, realizing Christ as Jesus, spoke of Moses' faith as serving the unrealized christ. In the same way, the prophets served the unrealized christ as they "made careful search and inquiry, seeking to know what person or time the Spirit of Christ within them was indicating as He predicted the sufferings of Christ." 4 The indwelling Spirit of God Himself within these people was leading them to follow His nature, His reality, the very substance of His being.

We see that the way the people listed in Hebrews 11 were saved was by responding to God's faithfulness. But that was a faithfulness that was still unrealized. They were responding to the image of God within them, the Law within them, the unrealized christ within them. They were "looking forward to the city with foundations, whose architect and builder is God." 5 They were serving the faith within them which was the substance of what they hoped for. The faith that they knew they knew was the evidence of things not seen.

So to say that faith is the acknowledgement of God plus saying a few prayers misses the point. Faith is the substance of God's heart. When we see Jesus, we see the faith we know we know.

One Faith

We say we are saved by faith, yet we are faithless to that faith. The image of God is within us, yet we are faithless to that image. The Law is written on our hearts, yet we are disobedient to that Law. Abraham, like us, was faithless to his faith. So when the scriptures say that Abraham, and we ourselves by inference, was saved by faith, the question arises: Is that faith something that Abraham did, or that we do? Or is it the faithfulness of God at work in us to which we are faithful or faithless?

To guide us toward an answer, let's look again at Hebrews. The writer of Hebrews describes the creation of faith in man, saying that Jesus Christ is the author of our faith. 6 The common image of God in every man, the common moral Law, is the inescapably universal faith that Jesus authored. This is the one faith Paul talks about when he writes of "one Lord, one faith." [7] *So when we speak of one faith, that faith is Christ.* Whether a person chooses to believe it or not, that faith is the reality, the nature, the being, the *substance* of God.

Faith is the reality, the nature, the being, the *substance* of God.

In this sense, Buddhists, Hindus, Jews, and Muslims, as well as Christians, have but one eternal faith written in their hearts: christ. Buddhism, for instance, sees religion as man's effort to do good morally toward one's neighbor. That is the outworking of their "faith." Yet any Buddhist knows that he cannot be faithful to his "faith." This question, "Are you faithful to your 'faith'?" has the same validity in the context of each man's religion, whether it is Christianity, Judaism, Hinduism, Buddhism, or Islam. No one can say, "Yes, I am 100% faithful to my 'faith'." Even the atheist acknowledges a sense of right and wrong. All confess that they violate the Law of their nature. This does not have to be proved. It is a knowing that all men know.

No one can say, "Yes, I am 100% faithful to my 'faith'."

The faith to which all people will be held accountable is the Law written on every human heart. This one faith, based on God's Law within, God's image within, cannot be snuffed out by any philosophy. Yet this faith cannot be fulfilled or perfected except through the author of it. So in this way, there is but one faith. It is the unperfected faith in those who don't believe, or the perfected faith in those who do believe.

It is either the *unrealized* fullness of Christ or the *realized* fullness of Jesus Christ.

The Faith of Christ

The Protestant Reformation began with the understanding that man was not saved by his own works or karma, but by faith. This shifted the focus of Christian belief from the works of man to the *faith of man*. All the religions of the world accepted the fact that man must save himself by his own works (karma). But as we've seen, man's karma is always blemished by his own sin. So while that shift from karma to faith was good, and even essential, it still left the responsibility of action to man. Since then, Western Christianity most often has identified faith as man's "faith in Christ" rather than the "faith of Christ" in the Father. But the Scriptures speak of the "faith of Christ Jesus." [8] Reformation theology should have moved from the works of man to the work of God, and from the faith of man to the faith of Christ. Our faith *in* Christ is secondary in the work of redemption because of the faith *of* Christ. We are faithless; He is faithful. He is the divine perfecter of our faith. For this reason, we put our faith *in* Christ.

**Reformation theology should have moved
from the works of man to the work of God,
and from the faith of man to the faith of Christ.**

When we move from the:
    Works of man to the faith of man . . . . action still comes
                                                                        from man.

    Works of man to work of God . . . . .action is God's.

> Faith of man to faith of Christ . . . . action is Christ's, because man's faith placed *in* Christ becomes the faith *of* Christ at work in man.

Today we commonly speak of our faith with no other thought than that it is exclusively ours. Even so, the believer in Christ Jesus is equally aware that first and foremost our faith is a gift from God. But it is not like a package we might receive, physically detached from the giver, to be used in any way we please. We are not like toy cars that zip around by themselves until the battery runs out. If our faith were so detached from our Maker, we could take credit for the usefulness of the gift as a result of our own wisdom. But faith is no such inanimate, impersonal gift. Faith's guidance is God's gift. He is alive and works within us, if we choose to receive His guidance.

**Man's faith placed *in* Christ
becomes the faith *of* Christ at work in man.**

Being creatures of choice, we come under the power of that which we choose. I once heard Norman Grubb say, "What we take, takes us. What we choose, chooses us." For example, until you choose to take food, food cannot work for you. But when you take food, you come under its power, and it works for you. It becomes your bone and flesh. If you take poison, it takes you. If you "take a seat," the chair you sit in works for you. You have a trust relationship with the chair. In a similar way, we can choose, or take, sin. If we do, then the sin we take, takes us: "... everyone who sins is a slave to sin." ⁹ Or we can choose Jesus Christ. If we put our faith in Christ, then the power of His Spirit is released to work His will in us.

Notice what happens when we say that we "put our faith in Christ": What we take, takes us. Christ's faith becomes our faith, and our faith ceases to exist. Our faith converts completely into Jesus Christ, so that He is now our faith. We receive Him, and the power of His life goes to work in us.

We give Him our sin, He gives us His righteousness.
We give Him our old life, He gives us new life.
We relinquish our old spirit to Him, He gives us a new spirit.
We give Him our faith, He gives us His faith—faithfulness.

**Christ's faith becomes our faith,
and our faith ceases to exist.**

It is not we who work, but the Spirit of God who works in us *through faith.* Faith is not a thing, but a vibrant person working in us. So faith works, not us. We no longer have to "work up" faith or "pump up" enough faith, for Christ's faith becomes ours. "I have been crucified with Christ; and it is no longer I who live, but Christ lives in me." ¹⁰ We are our faith. When we receive Christ, we receive the faith WHO is Christ. We receive the faith OF Christ. Only in Him can faith be perfectly lived out.

It is the righteousness of God that saves; our righteousness is secondary and is really not ours, but is rather God's gift of love. In the same way, primary to our salvation is the "faith of Jesus," and our faith in Him is secondary. We are saved
by the righteousness of God

> by the work of God,
>> by the grace of God,
>>> by the obedience of Christ,
>>>> by the faith of Christ.

Our entire faith centers in Jesus Christ. He authored our faith. He perfects our faith. And He is faithful to that faith, which He authored and perfected in us. He is the incarnation of God's faithfulness, and that incarnation is the only way faith can ever be perfected in us. So our faith finds its fulfillment, its completion, its full righteousness in Him. He is the *fulfillment* of the faith that every person has in his heart. *Our faith, our faithfulness, is Jesus Christ.* That is the simplest definition of faith.

Our faith, our faithfulness, is Jesus Christ.
Faith is not the What, but the Who.

The Law of Faith

Without Christ, our faith is incomplete. When perceived as a command, it's called Law. That Law, expressed in our obedience and responsibility to it, is faithfulness. The faith, or faithfulness, within us calls for obedience, just as the Law within us calls for obedience. Just as the Spirit of God within us calls for obedience. Just as the love of Christ in us calls for obedience. All these are one and the same, the complete sum total of the other when we see them through Jesus Christ our Lord.

George McDonald wrote:

> Faith, in its simplest, truest, mightiest form, is to do his (God's) will in the one thing revealing itself *at the moment*. . . [italics added] [11]

We might add:

Faithfulness, in its simplest, truest, mightiest form, is to do God's will. Jesus Christ at His simplest, truest, and mightiest does God's will.

Think of the examples given to us in the book of Hebrews:
Abel *offered* to God.
    Noah *prepared* an ark.
        Abraham *obeyed* by *going*.
            Moses *left* Egypt and *endured*.
                Rahab *welcomed* the spies.
These people of God were faithful. They were obedient. *Yet it was God who was the author and perfecter of their faithfulness.*

Faithfulness belongs to Christ. As the divine factor of faith, Jesus Christ is the substance, the incarnation of God's nature, reality, being, and person. As the human factor of faith, he is man's response of obedience, trustworthiness, and constancy. Hence man is justified, reconciled to God, *by the faith of Christ.* This is true whether we choose to believe Him or not. For "if we are faithless, He remains faithful." [12]

When people try to save themselves by their own works of righteousness, they put their faith in their own works, their karma, understanding that the Law of cause and effect will render the reward of peace and release from suffering to whatever good actions they can do. But trying to be perfect by our own efforts brings only condemnation, the Law of sin and death. We know that the Law is at work upon man's actions: the Law of karma, the Law of cause and effect, the Law of sowing and reaping. Man's faithfulness is always incomplete without knowing Jesus as the Christ. Without Him, all is simply Law, and under Law no man is justified.

However, because Jesus Christ fulfilled the Law, the principle of Law no longer operates upon the works, the karma, of man but upon the faithfulness of the work of Jesus Christ. Paul calls this the "law of faith," stating that now the causational principle of Law does not modify human action, but the work of God: "Where then is boasting? It is excluded. By what kind of Law? Of works? No, but by a Law of faith. For we maintain that a man is justified by faith apart from works of the Law." [13]

So man is not saved by the works of the Law, or even by the works that the Law is producing in him. Instead, man is saved by the work of God and His faithfulness in Jesus Christ's obedience to the Law. For the Law of faith does not destroy the Law of works, but completes it. In this way, man is saved by the faith of Christ. He is the faithfulness of the Father incarnate. With this in mind, let us read again Galatians 2:16, 20 from the King James Version:

> Knowing that a man is not justified by the works of the law, but by the faith (faithfulness) of Jesus Christ, even we have believed in Jesus Christ, that we might be justified by the faith (faithfulness) of Christ, and not by the works of the law . . . . the life which I now live in the flesh I live by the faith (faithfulness) of the Son of God, who loved me, and gave himself for me.

This is divine love.
God perfects our faith and completes it
by the work of Christ.

Jesus Christ, being God in the flesh, perfectly obeyed the Law of karma. He became the Law fulfilled. So to embrace Jesus Christ is to

embrace the karma that His faith has achieved and continues to achieve for us. This is a *living* grace accomplished only by the *living* faith of Christ. For Jesus Christ is our:
>obedience
>>trust
>>>reliability
>>>>constancy
>>>>>steadfastness
>>>>>>assurance
>>>>>>>certainty
>>>>>>>>conviction.

The moment we believe in Jesus Christ, it is no longer our faith, but the faith of Christ in us. *His* faith, *His* faithfulness, *His* work, *His* power, and *His* authority work for us. As Paul wrote, "It is God who is at work in you both to will and to work for His good pleasure." [14] It is a fact that God is literally at work in us through Jesus Christ. He works out His own life in us, a task we could never do. This is divine love. God perfects our faith and completes it by the work of Christ.

**The cause and effect principle
now operates on the faithfulness of Christ.**

Our faithfulness is imperfect, but when we choose Jesus Christ, we take on perfect faithfulness, trading our faith and work for His faith and work. By choosing, the transfer is made willingly. We understand that we are no longer under the Law of karma, our works, but under the Law of faith. We are being saved by the faithfulness of the work of God in Jesus. This is called "the law of Christ." [15]

So we see that the causational principle of Law operates upon the faithfulness of Christ. His faithfulness is at work in us. God no longer sees our work directly. Instead, he sees the work (karma) of Christ fulfilling the Law and removing the old Law of karma so that we might be under the Law of Christ.

The Equation of Faith

Man's faith under the Law of karma does not meet the full requirement of the Law. But Christ's faith does. Jesus Christ is without sin. He is God-man. We are saved by His obedience, His faith, His righteousness, His life. So:

> Our faith is Christ.
> Christ is our faith.
> Our faith is the work of God.

Christ Himself is the cause, and His faithfulness works the effect in us: He was faithful, therefore we are faithful. He was obedient, therefore we are obedient.

This is all God's scheme and work from beginning to end. He has expressed this to us as a new birth of His Spirit, which works in us as:
> the image of God within us
>> the Law within us
>>> the Spirit of God within us
>>>> the love of Christ within us
>>>>> the faithfulness of Christ within us.

And now:
> God is our faith
>> Christ is our faith
>>> faith is in the heart of every man.

In the preface, I introduced the term *metonomy*, the use of one aspect of something in order to refer to the whole thing itself. Throughout this book, we have been viewing God's relationship with us as if it were a diamond, one beautiful gem with many facets, each reflecting a different quality. We have just seen one more facet of the beauty of a relationship with our Maker: faith. To appreciate it fully, we need the whole equation of faith, which says:

>Jesus = the Christ in us.
>>Jesus = the image of God in us.
>>>Jesus = the fulfillment of the moral Law in us.
>>>>Jesus = our mediator.
>>>>>Jesus = our salvation.
>>>>>>Jesus = our faith.
>>>>>>>Jesus = our life.

Each description has a meaning that relates to a different complexity of our human makeup and need. Each is an absolute essential. Most important,

>Each = Jesus. Jesus = all of them.
>In the End, they all add up to the manifestation of God's love, that "God may be all in all." [16]

Summary: Chapter 11

In its human factor, faith is:
    man's ability to find correspondence with God's heart and life.
    man's ability to respond to God.
    what enables us to will to trust and obey.
Faith is best translated *faithfulness*.
In its divine factor, faith is the substance, reality, nature, and being of
    God's heart.
Christ is the substance, reality, nature, and being of God.
Faith literally means Jesus Christ Himself,
    though to many people, it is yet unrealized.
All are faithless to their faith, but accountable to it.
Only the author of faith can perfect it.
So there is but one faith:
    unperfected in the non-believer,
    perfected in the believer.
Our faith is a gift from God; we cannot take credit for it.
If we put our faith in Christ, His faith works in us.
If our faith is not in Christ, it is incomplete, simply Law.
Jesus is the substance, the incarnation of God's reality.
Jesus' faith becomes our faith and our faith ceases to exist.
So the causational principle of Law now acts on the work of God.
Man is saved
    by the work of God.
    by God's faithfulness in Jesus Christ's obedience to the Law.

¹ Note: Christians have far too long given our beliefs too much prominence. We're unified in our *faith*, but divisive over our *beliefs*. The difference in our doctrinal beliefs has created factions among us and set us one against the other. Belief has even become the grounds for extending or not extending fellowship to one another. Such unkindness and narrow-mindedness is unheard of in the religious community of the East. They would never equate their ceremonies and rituals with the essence of truth or their faith. We've invested millions in our beliefs, building our communities and removing ourselves from the world we need to be reaching.

We need to loosen up. It is a very sad mistake to equate God with baptism, or Truth with the Lord's Supper. The institutions in Christianity are not "the Way, the Truth, and the Life." Jesus said plainly "I AM the way, the Truth and the Life." "I AM the door." God is Truth and there is no other Truth. When we preach the Truth, we preach Christ. Truth is personal. Rituals, ceremonies, the earth, and all things therein should never be equated with Christ, the Truth of God.

So Christians would do well to understand that their faith is Christ and that the ceremonies and rituals and doctrinal beliefs that we have created in our communities are only a means to our end who is Christ. Our beliefs need not override our unity: We believe in the divinity of Christ.

² Karl Barth, The Epistle to the Romans, trans. Edwyn C. Hoskyns, 6th ed. (London: Oxford UP, 1965) 109-111.

³ Hebrews 11:26, 27, NKJV

⁴ 1 Peter 1:10, 11

⁵ Hebrews 11:10

⁶ Hebrews 12:2

7 Ephesians 4:5

8 The King James version shows Paul referring to Christ's faith, as opposed to man's faith, three times: Romans 3:22, Galatians 2:16, 3:22. Whether to translate these verses as "the faith of Christ" or as "faith in Christ" is an old issue. The King James Version translates it "the faith of Christ." Theologians and scholars have differed and continue to differ on their views about this. If the Greek grammar is flexible enough to allow two grammatical expressions, translating the Greek word either "in" or "of," then it seems to me that it becomes a theological question. What is the theology of Paul in the contexts under consideration? It is to the revealed faith through Jesus Christ that we must look to determine whether we translate these passages "the faith of Christ" or "faith in Christ."

9 John 8:34, NIV

10 Galatians 2:16, 20, KJV

11 Harry Verploegh, ed., <u>3,000 Quotations from the Writings of George MacDonald</u> (Grand Rapids: Revell, 1996) 78.

12 2 Timothy 2:13

13 Romans 3:27, 28

14 Philippians 2:13

15 Galatians 6:2

16 1 Corinthians 15:28

PART TWO

The Truth You Know You Know

Interlude

The Final Exam

A Thai town off the coast of the Gulf of Siam

For awhile, I taught in a Bible Institute attended by students from many small villages. The Institute accepted students as young as 17 who had as little as a sixth grade education. Many of them had not studied for many years. For them to be allowed to come to a Bible school was a great challenge. They were quite nervous and very uncertain about their ability to study at this institute of higher education. All of them were Christians, though many were first generation Christians who had come from animistic or Buddhist homes and had little understanding of the Bible or of the life of Christ.

About 70 freshmen were enrolled in my class. I began our first meeting together by asking, "How many of you believe in Jesus Christ as the Son of God?"

They all raised their hands.

"How many of you believe that God loves you and cares for you and will forgive your sins?"

All of them raised their hands.

"How many of you are saved by the grace of God and cannot save yourself?" I asked.

Again, all hands went up.

"How many believe that Jesus Christ lived and died for us, carrying our sins to the cross so that we can have a hope for a resurrection from the dead to eternal glory, just as Jesus Himself did?"

All hands went up.

"How many believe that you have been born again of the Holy Spirit of God, and that you are a new creature in Christ, that the old man died and the new lives, and that the blood of Christ cleanses you from sin on a continuous basis?"

They again affirmed their belief by raising their hands and saying, "Yes!"

I said, "See? You know the whole Truth. If I stood here for a million years and taught you every day, I could not teach you one new Truth. You know the Truth already and have no need for anyone to teach you. The Spirit of God teaches you all things."

The students grinned at me. Some laughed.

"I can teach you the Bible," I said. "I can teach you about the books of Genesis and Psalms. I can teach you the books of the gospel of Christ. I can teach you Paul's letters to the Romans, the Ephesians, the Colossians, and his other books. I can tell you about Moses, Abraham, Isaac, and Jacob, about the miracles Jesus performed, about how He was crucified. But I cannot teach you the Truth. You already know all things, because you have been anointed of the Holy One of God who teaches you all things.

"Moses is not the Truth," I continued. "King David is not the Truth. Jerusalem is not the Truth. Peter and Paul are not the Truth. Only God is Truth. This Truth you already know 100%."

Then I had them read scriptures:

> But the Helper, the Holy Spirit, whom the Father will send in my name, He will teach you all things, and bring to your remembrance all that I said to you.
> John 14:26

> When the Spirit of truth comes, he will guide you into all the truth; for he will not speak on His own authority, but whatever he hears he will speak; and he will declare to you the things that are to come.
> John 16:13 RSV

I asked, "How much Truth did Jesus promise that the Holy Spirit would teach you?"

"All Truth," they said.

"How much of what Jesus taught will He bring to your remembrance?"

"All," they said.

"The writers of the New Testament did not have to go to college or to a school of higher education in order to write the most famous book in all the world," I said. "The Holy Spirit gave them what they were to say and write. How would you like to have such an understanding of the Truth of God as promised in these verses?"

"We would really like that," they said.

"For many years I, too, wanted such an understanding," I said. "But when I was a young man, my Bible teachers taught me that these promises were only for the apostles of Jesus. Then one day, God spoke to me through a passage in 1 John 2:20, 21, and 27:

> But you have an anointing from the Holy One, and you all know. I have not written to you because you do not know the truth, but because you do know it, and because no lie is of the truth . . . And as for you, the anointing which you received from Him abides in you, and you have no need for anyone to teach you; but as His anointing teaches you about all things, and is true and is not a lie, and just as it has taught you, you abide in Him.

"By the time John wrote this, most of the apostles, if not all of them, were dead. So John addressed his letter to simple Christians. He gives to them the same promise that he had previously recorded in the gospel of John when Jesus talked to His disciples face to face.

"The only thing that makes these promises seem unreal," I said, "is that we have changed the definition of Truth. Jesus said, 'I am the Truth. . . .' He said that if a person saw Him, that person had seen the Father. To see Jesus is to see the love of a caring heavenly Father. To be born of His Spirit is to receive the same understanding of God that Jesus revealed: 'God is love.' The life and teachings of Jesus show us what this love means. When you know Jesus and have been born of His Spirit, you have been anointed by God's cleansing love and grace. This is an eternal knowledge that does not change.

"So if we listen to His Spirit in every situation, at every moment, with every problem, we will know the loving, kind, understanding, compassionate answer to give. Sometimes we may not have the physical data or thoroughly understand the spirit of a person about whom we must make a decision, so our heart may be right and our decision wrong. But in any case, we know we ought to meet the problems of every day with honesty and integrity, just as God is honest. This is the Truth of which Jesus speaks. God is Truth. Jesus said, 'I am that Way; I am that Truth; I am that Life.' [1]

"So," I said, "tomorrow we will have a final exam on the Truth of God."

The students looked shocked and frightened.

I said, "You don't have to worry about this, for the Holy Spirit will guide you as you answer the questions."

The next day, I gave my students 125 to 150 questions to be answered yes or no, such as:

Did God create the world?
Did God do it out of love?
Does God love you?

Does God forgive your sins?
Does God have grace and mercy for you daily?
Should you strive to be righteous and holy every day?
Should you be kind?
Should you forgive your neighbor of his sins against you?
Should you lie?
Should you murder?
Should you steal?
Should you take your neighbor's wife and commit adultery?
Should you deceive another person for sexual gratification?
Should you be lazy?
Should you cheat on tests in school?
If I loved you as the life of Jesus Christ shows us how to love, would I do any of the evils listed above?
If I love you as Jesus has shown love, will I be willing to live for you, to help you, to lay down my life for you so that you may live?
If we so loved, would we make our world a better world?
. . .and so on

Such questions can go on into unnumbered thousands that apply to the particular situations we face in life. In every situation, the Spirit of Truth, the promised teacher, gives us guidance. He is faithful and will always advise us about how we ought to live. Paul said, "I count all things but loss for the excellency of the knowledge of Christ Jesus my Lord." [2] For the knowledge of Christ is a living, vibrant, guiding Truth. "Indeed, the word of God is living and active, sharper than any two-edged sword, piercing until it divides soul from spirit, joints from marrow; it is able to judge the thoughts and intentions of the heart." [3]

I was certain that Bible study would dynamically reinforce the Truth my students already knew. The Bible would prepare them for the challenges of life and show them how other great men of God, and even Jesus Himself, met life's challenges. But the point I wanted my students to understand was that increasing their knowledge of the Bible would not increase the Truth they already knew in their hearts.

---

[1] Paraphrase, John 14:6
[2] Philippians 3:8, KJV
[3] Hebrews 4:12, NKJV

CHAPTER TWELVE

How Truth Verifies Itself

When I first went to Thailand, I thought I had to teach the people new words that would describe the attributes of Jesus Christ. So I began to translate these words. "Do you have a word for goodness?" I asked.

"Yes," they replied. "Quam dii."

"Do you have a word for kindness?"

Again the reply, "Yes, goranaa."

"For righteousness?"

"Quam chaab thaam."

"Mercy?"

"Yes, metta."

"Sin?"

"Baap."

"But what about forgiveness?"

"Yes. Yoke baap tod bi sia."

"Redemption?"

"Tai baap bi sia."

"Ah! I'll bet you don't have this one: reconciliation!"

"Khun dii gap."

The Thai people had all the New Testament words concerning goodness, love, and grace, as well as words for evil and sin. But what they did not have was the knowledge of how to put the concepts together. They knew love, but they did not know that God loved them or that they could be reconciled to Him. They did not know Jesus.

Seeking Proof

I felt another pressure when I first arrived in Thailand: the need to prove that the Bible was the word of God. The people challenged me to give evidence that Jesus was born of a virgin, that He walked on water, healed the sick, raised the dead, and ascended into heaven. My proof for these events was the Bible. So I had to show that the Bible was true.

I soon learned that the Buddhists proved their beliefs in a different way. While they did claim, "Buddha said this or that," the foundation of what they taught was not based upon ancient scriptural documentation to which they thought everyone should conform. Though they did have scripture, they didn't try to prove things by their scriptures. In fact, the Buddha specifically taught against the use of scripture or theory or tradition as authoritative in establishing truth. So the Buddhists based their proof upon Truth itself. If they spoke of ceremonies, rituals, and traditions, they simply showed how these ceremonies, rituals, and traditions symbolized the absolute, universal Truth as they understood it. On radio, television, and in newspapers, Buddhists proudly asserted that theirs was not a religion founded on faith but on scientific truths that could be established by the Law of nature.

Meanwhile, I preached that Jesus was God incarnate, without sin. I told people that Jesus had demonstrated His authority by miracles. I proclaimed that He had been raised from the dead and lives, even now, as Savior of the world. But each of these points needed to be proved. How was I to do this scientifically or historically? I went to the Bible. However, since Buddhists would not accept scripture as proof, the Thai people did not believe the Bible as my proof. They found my message weak.

In those days, the Moody science films had been translated into the Thai language. These films showed scientific evidence for the existence of God. In one scene, a spider, spinning its silky thread, dropped down the face of a cliff to pick up a stone that weighed hundreds of times its own weight. The spider brought up the stone, built a nest around it, and then left the nest there. When the baby spiders hatched, they did precisely what their mother had done, though she was no longer with them. The film asked, "How did the baby spiders know to do this?" Another scene showed young birds following their parents' exact migration route from Alaska to Hawaii, weeks after the parent birds had left them. Again, the film asked, "How could this happen?"

To a believer in God, these animal behaviors are absolute proof of God. So I would show these films and ask, "Do you believe this demonstrates the existence of God?" The people would answer, "Yes." But they had placed this information into a completely different frame of reference. They defined God as the non-personal Law of nature, or the dhamma. They believed that the spiders and birds had accumulated their knowledge over thousands and thousands of rebirths. In a similar way, the people explained the talents of Beethoven or Albert Einstein, or others who had been born with extraordinary genius.

Eastern religions call this concept the transmigration of the soul, rebirth of karma into another form, or reincarnation. They laugh at Christians for thinking that people are limited to a mere 70 years in which to learn how to be perfect. They teach that only through many rebirths and reincarnations can someone gain the ability to live according to the dhamma and become enlightened.

I discovered that in order to communicate effectively with Buddhists, I could not rely solely on physical or historical proofs. Instead, I had to rely on the only thing a person knows with absolute certainty: that which is within him.

In the West, we believers have given the impression that the only way God speaks to the human heart is through the Bible. And we do find Truth in the Bible. But we already believe. So as we study the scriptures, we're looking for the Truth, the heart and character of God's love, in every parable and teaching, because we already know this Truth. We pray as we study, asking God to show us how to apply Truth to the various situations of our lives. However, when we see Truth in the Bible, we say the Bible revealed that Truth. Actually, God revealed it *through* the Bible. But the revelation was not from the Bible itself; it was from the incident that was recounted in the Bible. Do we believe because it is in the Bible, or because it is Truth? We believe, because it is Truth.

I believe the Bible. I believe that through the Bible God reveals His love as the caring Father of all mankind. I believe the miracles of the Bible: that Jesus walked on water, healed, and raised the dead. You'll never find any book in the world through which Truth is revealed the way it is in the Bible. When you read Jesus, you read the love of God. The unique revelation that God unveiled in Jesus is the heart and character of His love: His forgiving grace, mercy, and compassion. But I believed before I could even read very well. I've seen converts who have believed Truth, yet have never read the Bible. Their hearts confirmed that what they had heard was Truth.

Sometimes it seems that we have deified the Bible. We have used it to show what a person must believe and do. We interpret theological issues that we think we understand: total depravity, predestination, election, everlasting punishment in hell, and more. Then we try to legalize the New Testament as a total catechism that others must accept mentally and verbally before we will fellowship with them. Yet there have been many individual interpretations of the scriptures, resulting in hundreds of denominations that find it hard to agree on doctrinal points or even to fellowship with one another. Each denomination claims it has the "truth" based on its own interpretation of what the Bible says.

Sometimes it seems that we have deified the Bible.

God has divinely inspired and recorded His incarnation in Jesus Christ so that the message will not be corrupted, perverted, or altered in any way. Having a written New Testament prevented the corruptions of the gospels by Greek and Eastern philosophers. The Bible keeps the message pure, and the early church gave it a stamp of approval. That is, they "canonized" it. They accepted it as being representative of what Jesus' life and teachings really meant.

But when presenting the gospel of Christ, there is no need to refer to the New Testament. Nor is it needful to use the New Testament as the authority of the Truth of the gospel. God has planned and designed His creation of man in such a way that whether man is educated or uneducated, literate or illiterate, primitive or civilized, Truth revealed in Jesus Christ finds validation in the human heart. People simply recognize God's image of love because it is the image He has put within them.

God has planned for the Truth revealed in Jesus Christ to find validation in the human heart.

Never has Truth been dependent solely upon the Scriptures. Think of the literal millions of people who have believed, yet have never read a New Testament. First century believers came to Christ before the New Testament was written. Many illiterate people come to Jesus, even today. Yes, the Bible testifies that Jesus is the incarnate Son of God.

And for me, the Bible is the source that made me aware of the Truth, the heart and character of God's love that dwells within me. But the Bible is not the ground of Truth. The ground of Truth is the Spirit of Truth as He revealed Himself to the writers of the Bible, the Truth that every human heart can verify as the fullness of God's love. So when I speak to non-Christians, I may use the Bible, but not as primary evidence of Truth. I use it as another witness that shows how the New Testament writers taught, just as I do, about the Truth that resides within every heart.

The Focus of the New Testament Writers

The ancient Jews focused on proof. They demanded a sign. But their means of verification was different from Jesus' ground of proof. They wanted physical proof of all Jesus said and did. Instead, Jesus offered spiritual Truth. "I will send the Holy Spirit and He will bear witness to Me," said Jesus. [1] The apostle John wrote, "And it is the Spirit who bears witness, because the Spirit is the truth." [2]

Our faith stands upon the witness of the Spirit. The Truth of the Spirit, the heart and character of God's love, confirms to the human heart the historicity of the New Testament documents and the genuineness of the gospel records. Yet it seems to be a subterfuge of Satan to try to focus our thoughts on physically proving documents and historical records which can never be harmonized word for word. While we should be thankful for Christian scholarship which has verified that our documents are genuine and worthy of our trust, if we try to refute the critical scholarship which deconstructs the gospel message in order to prove it unreliable, we fall into a trap. Critical scholarship has absolutely no bearing on the infallibility and inerrancy of the Holy Spirit of Truth. Faith in Jesus' life is an act of the Spirit of God, not an act of historical research.

It is really quite amazing that the writers of the synoptic gospels felt so little obligation to give details and exact representations of what Jesus actually said. Neither Matthew, Mark, Luke, nor John show any compunction about being exact as to time, date, and circumstance in their accounts of the life and teachings of Jesus. Matthew walked with Jesus. John was one of Jesus' closest friends. Yet each of these disciples inserted words or thoughts into his writing that the other did not include. Why didn't they take pains to make sure that everything they wrote harmonized with the other disciples' accounts?

Evidently, the New Testament writers were not concerned with being cross-examined, as in a courtroom, over exactly when, why, and where. Scholars say that Matthew had access to Mark's writings. Luke had access to both of them. No doubt later they all had access to the work of the others. If this truly is the case, they definitely were not concerned over any unexplained differences in their accounts, for they could have easily brought all apparent discord into harmony. It is naive to think that the early church did not notice the statements that needed clarification. Yet we are expected to explain the New Testament writings in a way that removes all claimed differences.

However, the focus of the New Testament writers was on the universal Truth of God's love as seen in the history of Jesus' life. This is what verified the Truth of Jesus in their own hearts, and they believed it would reveal the Truth to others as well. The historical events they described were the forms that revealed His Spirit of Truth. These writers used parables, metaphors, and analogies to help the readers see the heart and character of God. The gospels are historic spiritual prose about Jesus and how He reveals the invisible mystery of God's love residing in the heart of man.

Yet the gospels are different from the world's folklore and from the myths and legends of the religions, for the gospels are witnesses to the heart of God. Many myths and tales of folklore witness the Truth of goodness, nobility, honor, sacrifice, and love toward one's fellowman.

But they make no allusion to God forgiving sins or to His grace toward all mankind, or toward God being the ultimate hero who would die for all people, doing for them what they could not do for themselves.

The New Testament writers, just like anyone who witnesses or preaches a sermon, were primarily concerned with Truth, the heart and character of God's love, as seen and realized in Jesus Christ. In essence, they were saying, "We writers have seen this Jesus. We have talked to those who walked with Him and ate with Him. Here is what He said. Here is how the story of Jesus began and grew after His resurrection. Here is how our idea of God was impacted and how our relationship with ourselves, God, and others was changed. By reading and hearing this message, you can be changed too."

The New Testament writers simply told the story of Jesus. They concentrated their entire writing not upon the small details of history acceptable under cross-examination, but upon the universal Truth that all people can verify in their own hearts.

So I do the same. All believers witness the story of Jesus' faithfulness on our behalf in the same manner. We present the message in the most appropriate way, the way that seems to bring the most clarity, and we hope the hearer will feel the beauty and power that resounds with the self-verification of the Truth of God's love. When I preach or dialogue, telling about Jesus, I lay no special claim to divine infallibility. More often than not, I don't even allude to the New Testament. After a few hours of witnessing the love of God the Father as revealed in Jesus, I see people repent, confess, and give their lives to God. Why? Because the life of Jesus is a message from the Spirit of Truth that finds correspondence in the human heart. People know full well that *I* am very fallible, but they hear past me to the Truth. People simply listen for the Truth, the heart and character of God's love, in what we say.

> We present the message as clearly as possible
> and hope the hearer will feel the self-verification.

Jesus spent three and a half years teaching people who were of different ages, came from different backgrounds, and had different problems. He probably had hundreds of subtle variations in the way He presented any point or parable. The gospel writers, in recording Jesus' teachings, did not limit themselves to a fixed phrase or way of expression. It is most natural that Jesus' words and expressions would vary from time to time. I myself have been preaching for over 50 years, and I do my best to vary the message. I get tired of saying the same thing the same way over and over again. Besides, witnessing to a Thai Hinayana Buddhist requires a different way of expression than witnessing to a Hindu in India or a Westerner from the United States. Though I love the Truth, there are an infinite number of ways to present it, and I can honestly say that it never comes out the same way any two times. Yet the core message of God's love and grace is always inerrant and infallible.

> The message of forgiving love
> is the very essence of God's heart and character.

Every person brings to God hurts, pains, confusion, and sin that need the forgiving grace and love that comes through Jesus. The message of forgiving love, of God Himself obeying the Law's demands, corresponds so accurately to the human heart, that we know it is the very essence of God's heart and character. That is inerrancy. That is infallibility. That is Truth. And that is the message the gospel writers conveyed.

The Authority of Jesus

Jesus Himself knew that the confirmation of Truth was always God's Spirit bearing witness with man's spirit. Even His miracles were not the ground of His being the Truth. Miracles were only an added witness to confirm Him to the human heart, to bring about the awareness of God being God. But many who saw the miracles did not believe. They saw physically, but they would not listen to the Spirit, God speaking to their hearts.

> "By what authority are You doing these things, and who gave You this authority?" . . . And Jesus answered and said to them, "I will ask you one thing too, which if you tell Me, I will also tell you by what authority I do these things. The baptism of John was from what source, from heaven or from men?" And they began reasoning among themselves, saying, "If we say, 'From heaven,' He will say to us, 'Then why did you not believe him?' But if we say, 'From men,' we fear the multitude, for they all hold John to be a prophet." And answering Jesus, they said, "We do not know." He also said to them, "Neither will I tell you by what authority I do these things." [3]

When Jesus responded to the Pharisees' question by asking another question, what was He trying to do? First of all, He was thrusting these leaders into an inescapable dilemma. Both the people and the rulers knew that John had testified that Jesus was the Messiah, "the Lamb of

God who takes away the sin of the world." [4] If the rulers accepted John's testimony, they had to accept Jesus. If they denied John's baptism, the people would be angry.

Second, Jesus' question forced the leaders to be honest about what was in their own hearts. It was a spiritual judgment they would have to make in front of the people. The common people were capable of judging, and had already made a decision in favor of John. Now it was up to the Pharisees to decide. If they answered wrongly, the people would know that these leaders had no desire for Truth. Truth is never a question of proving. It is always a question of accepting with the intention of obeying. The Pharisees were not interested in accepting or obeying. They wanted only to protect their position as the sole religious leaders.

Third, by directing the question to those who wanted to destroy Him, Jesus was acknowledging that the authority to decide Truth was a power and right of all people, even His enemies. Any seeker of Truth needs only to recognize that words or deeds correspond to the Truth he already knows in his own heart. Revealing this Truth is a function of the eternal Logos, the life and light of the world, which "...enlightens everyone...." [5] When Jesus asked the Pharisees about John's baptism, He was appealing to their hearts in which this light, this Logos, could verify Him and His teachings.

> **Jesus acknowledged that the authority to decide Truth was a power and right of all people, even His enemies.**

That day, as people watched and listened, they sensed the tension. They were aware that this was a moment of truth. Everyone knew that John had refused to baptize the Pharisees because of their insincerity and lack of repentance. Now the people waited for their rulers' response to see if the Pharisees really were seeking Truth. Surely the people smiled secretly, reading their leaders' hearts, for the Pharisees stood there stammering through a discussion of their dilemma in front of everyone. When the Pharisees finally answered, they chose to silence Truth. Jesus had successfully laid the leaders' hearts bare before the people.

Actually, when Jesus followed the Pharisees' question with His own, He was giving them a direct answer. In order to respond truthfully to Jesus' question, the leaders would have had to reach down into their own hearts. The same authority they would have called upon to find Truth at that moment was the exact answer to their question. God has set upon each of us the responsibility to be the final witness to eternal Truth.

**God has set upon each of us the responsibility
to be the final witness to eternal Truth.**

A Common Database of Truth

God has given to every man and woman the authority to discern what is true and what is false. People are able to hold each other responsible for truthful words and actions, because all people have one common database of Truth: the Spirit of Truth. As children of God, made in His image, people hold in their hearts the authority to prove Truth in what they hear from Jesus. So Jesus asks people to decide what's True by listening to God's voice within them. This is an individual, personal judgment, a judgment that comes from the heart. Each of us is the final witness for what's True.

Jesus relied on the image of God within each person to verify the

Truth. This is what gave the ring of authority to Jesus' teachings. Matthew concluded his account of the Sermon on the Mount by saying:

> The result was that when Jesus had finished these words, the multitudes were amazed at His teaching, for He was teaching them as one having authority, and not as their scribes. [6]

What had evoked such a response? Jesus had told about the relationship of man to God. He had said that a heart given over to God becomes humble and poor in spirit, meek, merciful, and pure. This heart hungers and thirsts after righteousness, strives to make peace, and is even willing to be persecuted. People who heard this message saw nothing to argue about. Jesus had just revealed the Truth, the heart and character of God's love.

The authority of Law was condemnation.
The authority of Jesus was the authority of love and forgiveness.

The people who heard the Sermon on the Mount knew that what Jesus had said was True: You give your heart to God, and He will reign in you and work in you to make you merciful, peaceful, and pure. They could see that man's relationship to God would be just as Jesus had described it. They heard the mercy and compassion of God in His message. When they compared Jesus' life and words to the hypocrisy of their priests, scribes, and rulers, the people could tell that Jesus carried authority, for He brought glory and honor to God. He spoke of:

God having mercy, not just man having mercy on man;
God forgiving, not just man forgiving man;
the glory of God, not just the glory that man may be able to gain;
a personal God of love, not an impersonal Law of karma.

The authority of Law was condemnation, requiring the impossible of man. The authority of Jesus was the authority of love and forgiveness

Even the officers who had been sent to arrest Jesus saw His authority. They returned empty-handed:

> The officers therefore came to the chief priests and Pharisees, and they said to them, "Why did you not bring Him?" The officers answered, "Never did a man speak the way this man speaks!" [7]

The chief priests and Pharisees exerted authority based on the threat of physical harm. However, the officers experienced a spiritual awe for Jesus that outweighed their fear of the Pharisees' power. Without a weapon, Jesus had radiated powerful authority. People heard the Truth when He spoke.

The Spirit of Truth Tells the Truth

As Jesus was then, so He is today. His authority reveals the holiness and beauty of God's love for humanity. Jesus taught that His authority and kingdom are not of this world. "The Spirit of truth, who proceeds from the Father, He will bear witness of Me," said Jesus. [8] Proof is spiritual, not physical.

When the rulers asked Jesus where His authority came from, in effect He turned around and said to them, "You tell me." For the Spirit of Truth was telling them Truth. They simply had to choose whether to accept it and admit it or not. We all have the same choice. For example, what does the Spirit tell you in answer to the following questions?

> "God loves you and eternally cares for you."
> Is this wisdom from God or from man?

"Love as I have loved you."
    Is that from God or man?

"The Good Shepherd lays down His life for the sheep."
    Is that from God or man?

How did you know the answers? The power and authority of Jesus' teachings comes from the fact that they embody the same eternal Truth that created people to be instruments of God's love. In Jesus' life and teaching, people can see and hear His desire to be an instrument of the forgiving grace that only God can bestow. The Law of karma and the natural Law of the universe, as well as human will and personality, are too weak to impart such beauty and life.

The nature of Truth is that in God there is no lie. Truth is supranatural. It is God! When Truth reveals itself to the human heart, it is known as having its source in God. Jesus said, "I am the Truth." [9] So when a person is witnessing, the essence of his witness is what he reports in content and spiritual value about Truth. The exact words Jesus spoke and the precise time and place are of secondary importance. Of primary importance is communicating the universal Spirit of Truth that Jesus' life conveys.

What literally happens when someone hears this message? The Spirit of God easily identifies it as being absolutely, beyond a shadow of a doubt, the identical Truth the listener knows in his heart. People hear the Truth, and they KNOW. They respond by giving their whole life into the Father's hands.

When I was 10 or 11 years old, my parents had been Christians attending church only about a year. At this time, I had not been taught a great deal about Jesus or the Bible. Yet I was sitting in church one night when my heart was touched by the Spirit of God. I knew that I was a sinner and had violated the goodness and beauty of His image within me. Though I could not have explained it at the time, I knew enough to break down and cry. Before the evening was over, I had become a Christian and had been baptized. That night, I told God that I would never sin again, and that I would be a preacher. Obviously I broke one of those promises. But since that time, I have never doubted God. I knew that I knew that I knew. Where was the proof? Indelibly imprinted on my heart.

Truth is universal. Its very nature is incarnate: God's Spirit is in all of us, teaching and guiding us. He is in every human heart and needs no proof. So the gospel message is the Spirit's message, which finds fulfillment in the historical person of Jesus. It is rooted in the mystery of the Truth of God's love.

People hear the Truth that they know, and the final witness is the confirmation that rises in their own hearts. Jesus is the Christ, the Son of God. The primary, though not exclusive, verification of this is the Spirit of Truth. Although God chose to reveal His Truth through the physical form of a human being, the confirmation of this is never what the eye sees or what physical data proves. The confirmation is always God's Spirit bearing witness with man's spirit, just as Paul wrote: "The Spirit himself testifies with our spirit. . ." [10] We know God's character, because:

> He wrote it upon our hearts,
>   He made us in His image,
>   He breathed into us His life,
>   So His Spirit may speak to our spirits when
>   we are willing to hear.

If a heart cannot hear the beauty of God's love, it is listening to a different voice.

The final witness to eternal Truth is the human heart.

1. John 15:26, paraphrased
2. 1 John 5:6
3. Matthew 21:23-27
4. John 1:29, NIV
5. John 1:9, NKJV
6. Matthew 7:28, 29
7. John 7:45-46
8. John 15:26
9. John 14:6
10. Romans 8:16, NIV

Vignettes

The Tibetan Temple

An American woman staggered out of a Tibetan Buddhist temple, ashen and shaken. "I did not know that this is what it was like," she said.

Watching her was a group of people who had come to pray for the nation of Tibet. Their leader, a young lady from New Zealand, knew what was happening without being told. The teachings of the Dali Lama had been gaining popularity in the West. The message seemed gentle, kind, and tolerant. The woman leaving the temple was a New Age adherent who liked what she had seen in the Western version of Eastern philosophy. She felt she could increase her understanding of this wonderful school of spiritual thought by coming to Tibet. What she found was very different: spiritual oppression, grotesque images, darkness, and an emphasis on the cycles of birth, death, and rebirth. The reality of it had overcome her. What she had found was not the Truth. It was not the image of God's love.

* * * * * * *

The Word "Salvation"

I was sitting in Starbucks with my book and computer, drinking a cup of coffee. A young woman in her late twenties sat down near me. We began to talk. The conversation turned to God and Jesus. The young woman told me she had been raised in a charismatic church and that the pastor's moral life had been quite bad. So she showed a great deal of resentment toward the church and was skeptical as she listened to my viewpoint. Yet she was willing to pursue the conversation about God, and to tolerate talking about Jesus. I felt that the conversation was moving along well. Until I used the word "salvation."

Immediately a deep anger exploded within her. She said, "Don't talk to me about salvation." Then she quickly excused herself and left.

I have not seen the young woman since then. I don't understand why this word "salvation" triggered such a response. But this encounter made me wonder: Do we write her off unless she communicates in our Christian terminology? Or is there another way to word what we are trying to say without destroying the message? If so, are we willing to make the change?

* * * * * * *

Outside Christianity, Looking In

"I don't mean to be mean to Jesus in my thoughts. . . .But I don't get how he hates so many millions of people and sends them down to Hell."

- from *True Believer* by Virginia Euwer Wolff

* * * * * * *

Too Rational

After I had witnessed to an older man, he said, "It would be nice to believe. I admire your faith, but I'm too rational and logical to accept it."

I wanted to dialogue further, but he was ill and too tired and weak at that moment to continue our discussion. I wanted to ask him in a joking manner, "Did you create the world?" When he answered, "No," I would have asked, "Do you have to prove it? No, it's just a Truth we know. Is it all right to murder, lie, and steal?" When he answered, "No," I would have asked, "Do you have to prove it? No. It's a Truth that springs from the heart. It's a spiritual Truth, and that's the most rational of all thinking."

CHAPTER THIRTEEN

Cultural Barriers

Right before our eyes, the United States has undergone a dramatic shift religiously, culturally, and morally. The growth rate of Christianity in the U.S. is at 0.7%, while Islam is growing at a rate of 1.7%, Sikhism at 0.8%, Hinduism at 2.5%, and Buddhism/Eastern religions at 3.2%. Looking at the statistics alone, we find that the United States no longer contains the greatest number of Christians. In fact, Africa and Asia combined have more than three times the number of Christians as the United States has. [1]

One cause of the religious-cultural-moral shift in the U.S. is the change in the make-up of the population. Each year, thousands of immigrants from Eastern and Middle-Eastern countries bring their own religions with them into the U.S. A second factor emerged over fifty years ago when Eastern thought began to permeate our society. Eastern philosophies became attractive in the religious climate that had formed due to generations of denominational bickering and due to the Protestant community's opposition to religious forms and ceremony. A third cause is affluence, which has not only brought secularism, but has also planted growing seeds of hedonism. Our self-absorbed, pleasure-seeking culture has even permeated the church. As a result of these factors, the United States has become a pluralistic society.

The Pull of Pluralism [2]

The theological implication of pluralism results in viewing Jesus as just another religious teacher equal to Buddha, LaoTze, Confucius, Mohammed, and the Hindu philosophers. Pluralism asserts that the core of man's uniqueness is the common revelation of goodness that must be expressed in all human situations; that the human scene needs nothing more than for man to be good, compassionate, merciful, and righteous. As long as this is the accepted foundation, what one may say about God is irrelevant: A person can worship Jesus Christ as God, or the Buddha as God. God can be personal to you, or non-personal, or expressible as the "It" or Brahman or Nirvana or Allah. It makes no difference in pluralism, for the divine is simply love expressed as a common brotherhood living together in justice, peace, forgiveness, kindness, tolerance, and non-judgmentalness.

The kernels of truth in the previous statements are what gives pluralism its strength and dynamic appeal in our current culture. Pluralism popularizes goodness and kindness and tolerance to one's fellowman. In doing so, it appeals to the Truth of the image of God stamped in every person. The common denominator of ethical and moral values is on every heart. Whoever our Maker is, He has instilled this moral Law in each person.

Pluralism popularizes goodness, kindness, tolerance. In doing so, it appeals to the Truth of the image of God stamped in every person.

Pluralism rightly states that all religions teach universal Truths: speak honestly, be kind, be merciful, and so forth. Knowing that all people are under the Law of nature, we can expect this common ground. The goal of pluralism is for all people to receive each other in tolerance and respect. However, from a pluralistic perspective, what's true for one person may not be held as truth by another. So in the name of tolerance and respect, pluralism effectively bypasses one person's judgment of another in any area, including sinful behavior.

Pluralism has rightfully stood on the universality of the moral Law, but has turned a blind eye to the sin that plagues mankind. The sin of the world will always blind "the minds of unbelievers, so that they cannot see the light of the gospel of the glory of Christ, who is the image of God." [3] What pluralism cannot see is that sin is active and alive and life-controlling. Sin is a betrayal of self, others, and God. So tolerance and respect cannot bring about the unity and peace they seek. For when each person decides for himself the spiritual matters of right and wrong, he always brings biases, moral weaknesses, and hidden agendas into the process. This prevents the unity of lifestyle that pluralists desire. Only God's love revealed in Jesus can bring about true unity.

Philosophy does not demand a verdict, but theology does.

At this point, Eastern philosophy stumbles. It embraces the concept of love and the idea of knowing God, but it rejects the deity of Jesus, which pits philosophy (concepts and ideas) against theology (which deals with active Faith). Philosophy does not demand a verdict, but theology does. The philosopher is free to accept any kind of thought. After all, he is only philosophizing. He does not have to act or make moral decisions. He can embrace an idea or not, as he sees fit. He can view sin as an action or karma that simply brings about a distasteful or painful effect. On the other hand, theology sets up a relationship to a personal God. The one who believes in a personal God must make moral decisions and act upon them, because viewed theologically, sin is an offence against one's Maker.

Popular Voices

Our pluralistic nation is being saturated with Eastern philosophy. We know it as New Age thinking, but it is simply a Westernized Hinduism with some Buddhism thrown in. By nature this philosophy is adaptable, so it changes its language to match ours, replacing many gods, for example, with our one word "God" and using words like "love," "forgiveness," and "redeemer." Although some New Age adherents readily admit that Jesus is *one* of the gods, as a whole they have a problem with the divinity of Jesus, because if Jesus is the Divine One, then God is personal and intimate, and sin is exposed.

We can see New Age thought expressed in many of the educational programs on television and in the writings of prominent New Age scholars. These teachers have shifted subtly from the Eastern terminology of the Unknowable, the Unreachable aspect of Supreme Brahman to the English word "God." In so doing, they allow the hearers to unconsciously carry over whatever understandings they have of God. "God" is then spoken of as the Energy Source, a cold, impersonal "It." God ceases to be a loving Father desiring a personal relationship with His creation.

**The one who believes in a personal God
must make moral decisions and act upon them,
because viewed theologically, sin is an offence against one's Maker.**

When a Christian hears New Age philosophers use the word "God," he projects the Christian concept of God into it. The New Age speakers want us to do that, and that's how people get drawn in. We think they are saying something we believe. But they are not. They are dealing with the impersonal. And you cannot offend the impersonal, for it has no heart to offend. However, the minute they depersonalize God, they set themselves under Law.

Though New Age philosophers reference God as the non-personal Source or "It," they still say that this Source is somehow real and knowable. This is an example of the kinds of contradictions you will hear in this philosophy if you listen carefully to what they say. In their minds, all springs from the Energy which fills all. By this, they mean that "all is God." They stress that healing and miracles become possible by plugging into the Energy, which finds its source of strength and beauty residing within each person. So actually they are saying, "We are God."

New Age and pluralistic philosophy have gained a broad base of popularity and acclaim, even among people of the Judeo-Christian heritage. New Age teachings have been endorsed by people of prominence and influence in our society: well-known television personalities, religion professors at major universities, doctors and researchers at major medical schools, political figures, priests, nuns, and rabbis. Part of the broad appeal of these New Age and Eastern thinkers is that they have effectively brought God into science, while many in Christianity have set themselves against science. Another part of their appeal is the way they neutralize sin and open the door for people to sin without calling it "sin."

On another front, skeptical historical scholars are trying to disprove the Bible and the historicity of Jesus Christ. Advancing scientific discoveries in areas such as quantum physics, anthropology, and psychology have become tools in the hands of skeptics to reinforce the concept of the beginning and development of man apart from God. Add to this an emerging atheism, and we find even more opposition to Christianity. [4]

A Different View of Love

Many people in our society now use the word *love* to mean

kindness or compassion. Kindness is a virtue that is part of love, as is compassion or thankfulness. Love is respectful. But respect does not necessarily imply love. One can be kind, respectful, and tolerant for selfish reasons, hoping to gain prestige, social status, or economic increase, or to win an affair with an attractive person. People give and receive kindness easily, because kindness soothes the heart from the anxieties of the world. It can heal certain pains and troubles of life.

However, by turning a blind eye to the other virtues of love, such as truthfulness, holiness, and justice, kindness can be destructive to a person's well-being. For example, kindness can be so "kind" that it will not point out a person's destructive or immoral characteristics that will end up bringing sadness and heartache into that person's relationships. Such loving honesty, or "tough love," in our present culture is seen as intolerant and condemning. Yet when kindness ignores all the other virtues of love, it can be a tool of the devil. So yes, love is kind. But kindness is not necessarily love.

Neither is sex (Eros) necessarily love, any more than eating food is love. Eating in order to keep one's body strong and healthy can be an expression of a grateful love of life. But gluttony does not express love toward one's own body. Instead, it expresses uncontrolled lust and desire. In a similar way, sex can be an expression of love, but sex can also be devoid of love. It can be an act of hatred. It can be rape. It can be an expression of uncontrolled, undisciplined lust. So when we speak of the love of God, physical gratification has no part in the definition.

However, when we say the word *love* in our culture, people may interpret the word as only kindness, compassion, or tolerance. Or they may interpret it as sex. In any case, we should be aware that saying the word *love* does not necessarily evoke the thought of God or the fullness of His love. It is the cross of Christ that demonstrates the pinnacle of the definition of love.

A Changing View of Sin

To sin means to fail to be as loving, righteous, and good as God the Creator. He is the standard, the Mark of perfection, the image in us that we try to live up to. He is Love. Sin is missing the Mark, failing to live up to the standard of Love. However, the word *sin* has fallen into disfavor and has become a distasteful word to our pluralistic culture, which shares the Buddhist approach: Instead of being "sin," a particular act is "inappropriate" or "unworthy." This alleviates guilt and soothes the conscience. So pluralism has become perhaps the greatest solution men have found to neutralize, on their own, the condemnation of sin and to allow the circumstance of the moment to justify what they want to do in the long run.

C. S. Lewis pinpointed this growing trend 40 years ago:

> When the apostles preached, they could assume even in their Pagan hearers a real consciousness of deserving the Divine anger . . . . It was against this background that the Gospel appeared as good news. It brought news of possible healing to men who knew that they were mortally ill. But all this has changed. Christianity now has to preach the diagnosis — in itself very bad news — before it can win a hearing for the cure. [5]

The heart of God is love, a testimony to the fact that He is personal. But New Age philosophy denies God's personal nature, which allows man to construct his own image of a non-personal God, a God who is anything man wants Him to be. Thus the standard is eliminated. If the standard is gone, a person cannot miss the Mark, for there is no Mark at which to aim. It's true that New Age philosophy espouses the Eastern philosophy of "Do good. Seek good. Reap what you sow." This sounds like a proper and right goal. But "good" is whatever the individual person perceives or says is good.

If each individual decides for himself what is good and what is not, then the placement of the Mark is at the mercy of man's opinion. It's as if the bull's eye is constantly being moved. Yet if people do not identify sin and its consequences, sin becomes equal to goodness.

The equality of sin and goodness is exactly what some New Age philosophers teach in their books and lectures. One of these teachers defines sin as a wrong that leaves an impression, so that if the act doesn't leave an impression, it's not sin. Or if you forget the impression, it's not sin. He claims that God (who is impersonal, an "It") sees sinners and saints in the same light and sees all actions as equal, so he advises his readers that the goal is to embrace the idea that there is no dual system of good and evil. Thus people can break free from the bondage of good and bad actions. Eventually, he says, those who accept this philosophy will realize that they never did wrong to begin with. 6

**If man could achieve goodness on his own,
he would have done so by this point in history.**

Another popular New Age teacher emphasizes goodness and encourages people to live clean, wholesome lifestyles. So he recommends that a person make contact with the divine source of energy, the divine "It" that makes up all things. He describes the supreme energy source and man's heart as a seamless, wireless network that is turned on 24/7. 7 The Christian, too, believes this, knowing that God is the Supreme Energy Source who is in constant contact with us, unless we choose to break the contact. What this New Age philosophy seems not to understand or teach is that sin breaks the contact. Sin that is alive and real in people's hearts prevents them from being able to call on the Supreme Energy Source as a loving, caring, gracious Father who is always there to help. Those who adhere to New Age teaching cannot speak of God in personal, intimate terms because moral Law, if they were really faithful to it, would identify and condemn sin.

If man could achieve goodness on his own, he would have done so by this point in history. But we still have cheating and lying, divorce and greed, wars and abuse. Man has proved himself to be a poor governor and judge of this world. This is the result of the strength of sin, for it has the power to separate us from God.

> **Sin has power because of our worth.**
> **If we had no worth,**
> **God could just say, "Never mind; forget it."**

Sin has power because of our worth. If we had no worth, God could just say, "Never mind; forget it." But sin separates us from the Mark, the standard, Divine Love. For the wages of sin is separation, death. Life is union. Death is separation. Sin separates us from that inner goodness, the inner "ought" that we ought to do

However, *sin is not a problem for God.* From the beginning, He knew sin would exist. He knew we would miss the Mark. Some sins are more unnatural than others and have a more devastating effect on us (though the wound heals, the scar is still there). Yet what concerns God is that we come closer to Him. His love is available to take care of our missing the Mark. God's love through Jesus really means that He:

    does not ignore our sins,
        does not pretend sin does not exist,
            but recognizes sin,
                and takes away sin's power

by receiving sin's consequence of death Himself,
cleansing us of sin
to perfect in us the Love that transcends our
highest thoughts.

**God's love is available
to take care of our missing the Mark.**

None of the New Age teachers reaches deeply enough to find Truth. But they've proved to be excellent communicators by adopting Christian expressions of God, and by being very low-key in expressing their belief in reincarnation into other living forms based on the Law of karma. Their focus on freedom and goodness rings with Truth to the human heart. Compared to their presentations, most Christian media does not communicate to the unbeliever. The Bible, which is meaningless to the non-Christian, is constantly used as the proof of what is being said. The Christian message comes across as combative, angry, and strident. So a negative chord sounds loud and clear before the positive Truth ever comes out. Operation World states, "Christians have generally proved singularly ineffective in communicating the gospel in a relevant and winsome way to secular, post-modern culture." [8]

We must realize that in our society, educated people age 45 and younger have been culturally trained to receive a form of teaching that is different from the preaching of the old-fashioned tent revivals. The times are different; the culture is different; the educational level is different. Our message is not wrong, but we must learn to present the message in a way that is self-verifying to the listener. Our own culture presents us with enough barriers to overcome. We must avoid creating more. The next chapter will point out some of the barriers that we ourselves inadvertently set up.

1 Patrick Johnstone, Jason Mandryk, Robyn Johnstone, <u>Operation World 21st Century Edition</u> (UK and USA: Paternoster Lifestyle, 2001) 1-32.

2 "Pluralism is conceived to be a proper characteristic of the secular society . . . in which there is no officially approved pattern of belief or conduct." Lesslie Newbigen, <u>The Gospel in a Pluralistic Society</u>, Eerdman's, 1989, 1.
"Pluralism . . . refers to the acceptance of many groups in society or many schools of thought in an intellectual or cultural discipline." <u>Microsoft Encarta Encyclopedia 2001</u>, s.v. "Pluralism."

3 2 Corinthians 4:4, NIV

4 According to <u>Operation World</u>, 9.4% of the U.S. population is non-religious (page 658).

5 C. S. Lewis, "Human Wickedness," <u>The Problem of Pain</u>, (New York: Touchstone, 1996) 49.

6 See the works of Deepak Chopra, specifically <u>How to Know God</u>.

7 See the works of Wayne Dyer.

8 <u>Operation World</u>, 14.

Interlude

Hill Tribal Village

Mountains loom before me as I, with a group of tribal Christians, trek to a remote animistic village. We start our long climb by truck, but end up on foot. At last we arrive at a compound surrounded by broken fences originally intended to guard the deteriorating bamboo buildings with their decomposing leaf and grass roofs. Refuse litters the houses and walkways. Dogs are skinny. Pigs are bony. They look like they have not received their daily diet of chopped banana stalk. It has obviously been some time since the water buffalo have been led into the forest for their daily grazing so that they will have strength to plow the fields.

As we walk through the village, we pass a specially designated long house. The unmistakable stench of opium and marijuana drifts from this hut into the air around us. We know what we would find if we made the short climb up a bamboo ladder into the smoke-filled room. Filthy, unkempt men and women lie all over the floor, smoking from their handmade bamboo opium pipes. Children three to ten years old sit beside some of the smokers, taking a free puff whenever they want.

Generally, the smokers are not happy to be engaged in this occupation. Only the physical addiction and the frustration of daily living drives them to it. Their habit is costly. They must plant their fields with rice in order to have enough to eat throughout the year. Smoking opium takes whatever free time they have in the evenings. The hangovers of the following mornings often make them sleep instead of going to work in the fields or hunting for food. By neglecting their labor, these villagers only increase their misery and the fear of the demons, which they perceive as bringing about their troubles in the first place.

To these evil spirits, the villagers will sacrifice their chickens, pigs, or water buffalo in order to heal whatever sicknesses come upon them. All of this makes ready cash scarce. In order to find money, they will sell their children to white slave peddlers who visit them periodically looking for girls and young men. Some villages make money by building special brothels to entertain and serve tourists, providing them with opium, marijuana, and sex. Often there is not a girl above the age of eleven in the village, because all the older girls have been sold into prostitution. The faces of the remaining children reflect a sense of fear.

Usually no one will look at us or speak until we find the headman or shaman. But we have guitars, and we sing songs that the children can pick up quickly. "God loves you, and I love you," we sing. As we sing the verse over and over, the children begin to come. Soon they are laughing and joining in. We are like television to them, good entertainment. The women come next. The men at first only peer out from the doors and windows. Eventually, though, the men come closer so they can hear more clearly.

We ask where the headman is, and we go to his home. He sits cross-legged in front of an earthen hearth, and we join him there. The women and children crowd in, and a few men may come. The headman makes himself a cigarette. After a brief salutation, he asks us why we have come.

"We have come to tell you about the love of God," we say. "We know you believe in God."

Actually we know that the tribal people may believe in two gods, one male and one female. These people are animistic, which means they "worship" demons or spirits. But they do not love the demons. Instead, they fear and placate them. For example, if a man comes home sick, he will go to the shaman and tell him about the illness. The shaman may ask him which tree he stopped to urinate on in the jungle. Then they will take some glutinous rice, some fruit, and maybe some whiskey to offer up to the demon of that tree so the demon won't make the man sick anymore. If the wife is sick, the husband will go to the shaman and maybe offer up a water buffalo.

So we ask the headman, "Do you know about the love of God? Do you know God loves you?"

The shaman takes a puff of the cigarette. He looks at the celing, then spits through a crack in the floor. "No. I don't know that God loves me."

"Do you know that God will forgive your sins?" we ask.

He takes another puff. "No, I don't know that God will forgive my sins. But maybe he could. . ."

"Did you know that God will send His Holy Spirit so that you will have a whole new spirit and be worthy to be called the child of God? Then you will not be afraid of the demons anymore. The Holy Spirit is more powerful. He will make the demons flee. You sacrifice water buffalo and chickens to appease the demons. Do you know that God gave His Son as a sacrifice for your sins so that there will be justice in washing your sins away? Then the sin you now love, you will hate. The good you now shun, you will do."

"I did not know that," the headman says.

We begin to sing a song. "He paid a debt He did not owe. I owed a debt I could not pay. I needed someone to take my sins away. . . Christ Jesus paid the debt that I could never pay." Twenty or thirty people are crammed into the hut listening to us. We explain each phrase: "*He paid a debt.* What debt? *He did not owe.* Why did He not owe it? *I owed a debt I could not pay.* [1] Why could I not pay?"

Because the villagers fear spirits and try to appease them, we explain, "Notice this new song. Our sin is taken away, and we have been born of the Spirit of God, the Holy Spirit. We have not come into this village to buy your daughters and your sons. We have not come to buy your opium or to sleep with your women. We have come with a different spirit, the Holy Spirit of God. Look! This is a Spirit of joy. A Spirit of goodness. Have you ever heard of this Holy Spirit?"

"No," they say.

"Do you know how to have Him come down and dwell in you?"

"No," they say.

"This is the good news that we bring. For God will give his Holy Spirit to all those who will receive His love. This forgiving love is revealed in His Son Jesus Christ. He will drive out the evil spirits that are in you and will bring you joy. He will cleanse you of your sins, so the sickness of sin will not take over your village as it has done. This Spirit is not a spirit of fear, but of thankfulness and joy in the love of God. When this Holy Spirit comes into you, it is possible for you to come into the Kingdom of God and let Him reign in your life. And if you sin again, which you will, He will give you forgiveness and cleansing, allowing you to come back to Him again, all new."

---

[1] "He Paid a Debt He Did Not Owe" w/m by Ellis J. Crum, Kendallville, IN, 1979. Arr. © Copyright 1979 "Special Sacred Selections," by Ellis J. Crum, publisher; Kendallville, IN, 46755 International copyright secured. All rights reserved. All arrangements with these words or this theme are illegal unless authorized by owner.

The Truth You Know You Know

CHAPTER FOURTEEN

The Barriers WE Build

We must simplify our message so that there is a true understanding of the good news about Jesus. As we have seen in previous chapters, we can present Truth to even the smallest child with the belief that he is capable of receiving or refusing it. We trust that the Spirit of God will confirm Truth to the image of God within each person, including the New Age follower and the skeptic. However, even though our intentions are good, we ourselves can get in the way of the message of God's love. What are some of the stumbling blocks that we inadvertently set up?

1. **Becoming offended when the world questions and investigates our claims.**

We live in a marvelous world of technology. The internet can circum-navigate the earth in a matter of seconds. Chemistry, astronomy, physics, geology, anthropology, and philosophy generate great databases of reliable facts. Massive populations in many nations are now literate and are increasingly able to tap into these resources. From this cauldron of sources, people seek trustworthy information.

At the same time, among the more highly educated people, there is a growing skepticism about the theological positions held by the Christian community as a whole. Many people have serious and valid questions and do not easily turn a deaf ear to contradictions among

Christian views or claims that seem outlandish to them.

◦≈◦

> **Without the incarnation, we cannot perceive
> that God cares so much that He would fulfill all of love's
> demands even to the point of dying for us.**

◦≈◦

Christian assertions concerning the Bible as absolutely perfect and accurate in all matters and concerning Jesus as God in the flesh are serious claims. Because there is a true need for people of science to sort out fact from fiction in our world, it is only natural that believing people and skeptics alike take up the challenges of such great claims and apply to them the tools of scientific and historical research. So we should not be offended when people question, for Truth has nothing to fear from any investigation. However, if we get drawn into trying to prove historically or scientifically what can only be proved spiritually, we get lost in a maze of debates, and our focus shifts away from the Truth about Jesus. For instance:

<u>Trying to prove the historicity of Jesus.</u>
No one living today can touch the historical Jesus in the flesh. It is not historical proof that verifies the incarnation of God as man. Instead, it is the incarnation that verifies the historical reality of Jesus. Without the incarnation, we cannot perceive that God cares so much for us that He would fulfill all of love's demands even to the point of dying for us. In other words, the incarnation of God as man is the only window that allows us to see how much God loves the world and how gracious and personal He is to redeem and recreate the human spirit. What the Spirit of Truth confirms to us about God proves that the history is true.

<u>Deifying the Bible</u>.

I do not want in any way to take away from the dynamic authority of the Scriptures. When we read them, we hear and feel the love of God. We are drawn into the nearness of God's heart and know Him to be our Father. The Scriptures carry the divine loftiness of true spirituality.

So the Bible must be studied and taught in a vibrant way that seeks answers to the constantly shifting philosophical attacks against God's glory, deity, and holiness. Youth must be taught biblical lessons, and adults must not forget them. But we must keep our view of the Bible and its very valid place in balance. I believe in the Bible. I believe it teaches God's Truth. I believe it is the greatest living miracle. God, speaking through the Bible, demonstrates that He is a living active Presence. However the church has deified the Bible. We have made it our God. With the Bible held high as the one and only word of God, we burden ourselves with an onslaught of attacks from endless quarters. We then get sidetracked into trying to prove the Bible. But there is no way that we can verify all the Old or New Testament happenings. As we saw in a previous chapter, the only claim to absolute perfection and infallibility that can be ascribed to the Bible is the revelation of God's perfect love. This love is shown in the life of Jesus Christ. That's the only thing the early Christians had to defend. They had no Bible. They simply told the story. Yes, they had the Old Testament, but even it was valid as a teaching tool only to those who were Jews or their proselytes. So without a Bible as we know it, Jesus and his disciples taught, and many people responded. For the message is not True because it's in the Bible. It's in the Bible because it's True.

∽

**The message is not True because it's in the Bible.
It's in the Bible because it's True.**

∽

In today's world, there are still many illiterate people. Some live in remote areas and have no concept of the printed word. Using a book as the proof of Truth makes no sense to them. A missionary who worked in Papua New Guinea told me about a visiting preacher who spoke to a group of illiterate villagers. As he talked, he held up the Bible. Afterward, one of the villagers picked up the Bible, turned it this way and that, and flipped through the pages with a look of curiosity. The missionary said, "We might as well have taken the Sears and Roebuck catalogue into the village. It would have meant more to the villagers, because at least it would have had pictures."

Even in today's literate societies, many non-Christians find the Bible to be a formidable book, difficult to read and hard to understand. In addition, they see the Bible as the Christian "rule book" and perceive the Christian position as, "Obey this book to the letter, or come under judgment." They also think the Bible is the Christian's strongest evidence for his belief. But as we have seen, this is not true. The Bible preserves the historical record with integrity. However, the strongest evidence is the Spirit of Truth witnessing to our spirits. Then what we read in the Bible confirms this witness.

So it is unreasonable to demand that people accept the Bible in toto as a prerequisite to accepting Jesus Christ. Once people hear the message and believe it, then they have a context for believing the Bible. For years, I have used the self-validating nature of the Truth to teach and witness the message of Jesus Christ. The message has spiritual authority, and once it is explained and taught without any particular reference to the Bible as such, it confirms itself. At that point, the Bible finds its validation in the believer's heart. In my experience, when people have accepted God's message of love, they ask me, "Where did you learn about Jesus?" I say, "In a book called the Bible." "Can we read this book too?" they ask. Their hearts and minds are ready to receive and appreciate the Scriptures. They want a Bible for themselves.

<u>Demanding that people believe the miracles recorded in the Bible before they can know Jesus Christ.</u>

I was riding by rail from Chiang Mai, Thailand to Bangkok. My seat on the train was opposite some German students who had traveled to Thailand to study tribal people in the hills near the Burma border. When they discovered that I had lived in that area and had worked with the tribal people for ten years, they became very interested. They asked what I did. I told them I was a Christian missionary.

One of the men, a tall, blue-eyed blonde, told me that when he was younger, he had thought about entering the ministry and studying theology. I asked him why he had changed his mind.

He replied, "If you are a Christian, you must believe the Bible and all the miracles that are in it: God parting the Red Sea, Jesus raising the dead, healing lepers, and giving sight to the blind. Christianity asks a person to believe and do too much."

I said, "In telling about Jesus, I don't feel it's necessary to prove that the Red Sea was parted, or that Jesus walked on water or raised the dead or healed the leper. Most of the Asian people whom I have brought to Jesus Christ in my life did not know all these stories. I simply tell the Thai people the good news of how beautiful God truly is. Not only does God have the power to create, but He also has the wisdom to bring all things together in perfect harmony through His immeasurable forgiving and redeeming love revealed in Jesus Christ."

If I had picked up the young man's gauntlet, I could never have proved these miracles to his satisfaction. The one thing I knew I could demonstrate to him was the self-verification of the gospel of Jesus. Miracles are not a problem once you have believed the love of God and have learned that He is *for* you, so concerned about you that He bore your sins. When a person believes in Jesus first, then he takes in the miracles.

<u>Getting sidetracked by trying to disprove evolution and other scientific claims</u>.

Some Christians seem to think scientific data and Christianity are mutually exclusive. This mindset is a trap that puts us in a stand-off with the scientific community. Evolution is the most visible example of this.

I believe God created the physical world and man. But for the most part, we Christians have turned away millions by the way we have presented our position concerning creation and evolution. The Bible states that God created. Yet how we humans and our physical world developed or didn't develop is not the important issue. The important issue is Jesus.

When we argue about evolution, we're beating an old tar baby, and every time we hit it, we get stuck more tightly with our backs turned toward the message of Jesus. Besides, our assertions about evolution don't ring with truth to non-believers.

Our message has to ring with reason and logic to skeptics, scientists, and non-believers.

I have found that when I enter into a discussion with someone over whether evolution is true or false, we never get to Jesus. So if the person mentions the Genesis account of creation, I just say that it was prehistory. No eye-witness recorded the event. Rather Genesis is an explanation of the beginning. The Bible is not a science textbook, but it is a logical book that says God is behind it all, reasoning, thinking, and loving. Adam and Eve accurately portray the heart of every man and woman in relationship to God. We all ate of the fruit and lost that relationship. The story embellishes deep spiritual insights that we truly need. Our focus is to avoid being caught up in the type of endless discussions that fill the secular world.

**When I enter into a discussion with someone
over whether evolution is true or false,
we never get to Jesus.**

Long before the idea of evolution ever arose, people understood that the Genesis account was prehistory. The important point is that our Creator has given us a common image and knowledge through which we can rationally know the greatest attribute we could ever have in any relationship: the kind of love demonstrated in the cross of Christ. The only thing we know with certainty is that when we see Jesus, we see the love we know we know: God incarnate. The Truth is proclaimed by knowing nothing "except Jesus Christ and Him crucified." [1]

Once again, we must not forget that the message of Jesus is confirmed by the Spirit of Truth bearing witness to the hearer's spirit that the gospel message is True. We must remember that people experience the Holy Spirit of Truth not by historical or scientific investigation, but by the heart of the Father whom Jesus revealed. Jesus promised that the Spirit of Truth would bear witness to Him. [2]

* * * * * * * *

2. Projecting an across-the-board condemnation of all other religions.

Jesus said that broad is the way that leads unto destruction and narrow the path unto life; many go the broad way and few go the narrow way. [3] This is not a statement of condemnation, but a statement of fact. People alone under Law always stand condemned by Law. However, using this fact to pronounce judgment on others only gives them the perception that Christians are hypocritical and condemning. Hypocrisy and condemnation are not doorways through which we can show God to others. Only a humble heart can reflect God's love, grace, mercy, and forgiveness.

But didn't Jesus condemn? Didn't He say that unbelievers would be cast into outer darkness where there would be the gnashing of teeth? [4] Passages like this are not pronouncing judgment upon people. Rather they are highlighting what the people already believed under the Law of karma. The Greeks depicted sin's evil effect by picturing Hades and miserable states of reincarnation. Eastern philosophies also had their concepts of hell and its different degrees of punishment, along with miserable states of rebirth or reincarnation. They all understood the axiom, "If there is no hell, let's live like hell." However, the greatest condemnation is to teach, "There is no forgiveness of sin. People *must* reap what they have sown."

Jesus did not condemn when He said, "Except you believe in me, you will die in your sins." [5] Instead, Jesus was simply stating a fact: Under Law, people must reap their sin. So instead of condemnation, Jesus was actually introducing the beautiful option: God loves you. He spoke the simple Truth about how the world must perish if it chooses to ignore the love and grace of God.

The German student who discussed religion with me on the train in Thailand made another insightful comment during our conversation. "Look at these Thai people," he said. "They are friendly and seem very happy. They are morally as good as anybody. Yet Christianity says they are lost in sin. It seems like Christians judge everybody else as wrong and only themselves as right. What makes Christian pastors any better than Buddhist priests?"

"I hear what you are saying," I said. "But I have been preaching and teaching for over 40 years, and my understanding is different from what you have stated. First, I do not believe that God loves the Christian one ounce more than He loves the Buddhist priest, or the Hindu, or the tribal shaman. I believe He loves us all equally, without partiality. I also believe that there are perhaps many Buddhist priests, as well as other devout Buddhists, who live more sacrificial lives than I do. Their lives are every bit as good as mine. I believe that God loves them for it.

"I simply preach about the love of God and His wisdom, which is far greater than any of the religions ever teach. In Jesus, God came to fulfill the demands of righteous living to which the moral Law guides us. To accept Jesus Christ is to accept God's life, to accept that power of love working in your life. This is not a message of condemnation, for God's love accepts all, His grace forgives our sin, and His life swallows up the death that is in the world. That is what I believe Jesus taught, and his disciples after him."

"I could believe that message," said the young man. "It is beautiful. If I had understood it that way, perhaps I would have been a minister."

The German student was right about the Thai people. Buddhists know what is right and good, and they teach it to their children. Like the young German man, they do not understand why we would condemn them. Why would a Christian take this hard position of condemnation? Because of his understanding of some of the scriptures from the Bible. For example, John 8:23, 24:

> And He said to them, "You are from beneath [under Law]; I am from above [under grace]. You [under Law] are of this world; I [under grace] am not of this world. Therefore I said to you that you will die in your sins; for if you do not believe that I am He, you will die in your sins." (NKJV)

Again, this is not a condemnation, it is a simple fact, one that the people knew.

We Christians often quote John 3:16. But John 3:17 is just as important: "For God sent the Son into the world, not to condemn the world; but that the world might be saved through him" (RSV). Jesus did not come to condemn. Yet we do exactly that. Our message to non-believers has been judgment and condemnation. As a result, they perceive themselves as righteous as we are, yet not as narrow-minded and dogmatic, for they project greater compassion and understanding toward others' differences, sins, and weaknesses than Christianity appears to do. Yes, there is condemnation. But the condemnation is from the Law, not God. As we judge and condemn others for not accepting Jesus Christ, what the non-believer hears is that Jesus condemned, when the very opposite is true.

The good news, the beautiful option, is that God does *not* judge the world. Instead, He appeared in the world to save man from the condemnation that already existed under the moral Law. He came to carry the sin of the world upon Himself. Jesus stated the reality known in every human heart. The condemnation is a self-condemnation, imposed by the Law of karma. The honor and glory of God is the grace that He has given. When grace is accepted, God is glorified and so is man. When grace is not accepted, God is not honored but is perceived as a tyrant in the hearts of mankind. This is the way the Law blinds people.

Author Madeleine L'Engle wrote, "We do not draw people to Christ by loudly discrediting what they believe, by telling them how wrong they are and how right we are, but by showing them a light that is so lovely that they want with all their hearts to know the source of it." [6]

* * * * * * *

3. Failing to see the beauty and truth in other religions.

The famous musical "The King and I" is based on the life of an Englishwoman named Anna Leonowens, who lived for a time in Thailand and taught the royal children. Here is her real-life description of Wat Pra Gaow, a temple in Bangkok:

> As often as my thought reverts to this inspiring shrine, reposing in its lonely loveliness amid the shadows and the silence of its consecrated groves, I cannot find it in my heart to condemn, however illusive the object, but rather I rejoice to admire and applaud, the bent of that devotion which could erect so proud and beautiful a fane in the midst of

moral surroundings so ignoble and unlovely, — a spiritual remembrance perhaps older and truer than paganism, ennobling the pagan mind with the idea of an architectural Sabbath, so to speak, such as a heathen may purely enjoy and a Christian may not wisely despise. [7]

Anna Leonowens saw the Thai people with the same eyes through which Paul saw the Athenians. [8] The Thai people were a worshiping, religious people, and Anna appreciated their religious efforts.

There has been no real concept among Christians in the U.S. that other religions teach any Truth. In fact, we often appear to despise other religions. One Christian man came to Thailand from the United States, carrying some American soil with him. He threw the dirt at the image of Buddha. The result was that he was deported for desecrating a Buddhist image. [9] Others have approached the idol, lifted their fists, and cursed the idol in Jesus' name. But Buddhists don't believe the idol has any power. They simply see it as a reminder to do good. When we exhibit scorn for their culture, we destroy any chance we might have to witness God's love to them.

We seem to fear that if we acknowledge that God's Truth is found in any way in these other religions, we are compromising, because they do not believe the Bible. Yet as we've seen, the Eastern religions emphasize love, compassion, and goodness. These beautiful qualities find their source in God. It is the *perfection* of these qualities that is found only in Jesus.

* * * * * * *

4. Sounding exclusive when we say that Jesus Christ is the only way.

It is difficult *not* to sound exclusive and self-righteous when we teach about Jesus, for we are sharing with people something we know and assume they don't know. But if we speak in such a way that people feel we are judging them, our beautiful message of love transforms into a message of condemnation. Then the only thing people hear us saying is that Jesus is the ONLY WAY. All we're really saying is that the only way to escape our karma is for God to forgive it. But people don't understand the ONLY WAY, because they see Jesus as just another religious teacher like all the others who teach goodness, kindness, and righteousness. Our exclusive claims sound arrogant and damning. When this happens, we've introduced the name of Jesus too quickly.

On what grounds, then, do we teach about Jesus? On grounds that do not need proof. God communicates and verifies His image and character only in incarnate ways. He has written His image upon every human heart. So His Spirit confirms the Truth to people's spirits if they have "ears to hear and eyes to see." [10]

Jesus does not exclude anyone. He loves the whole world. Love is inclusive. So when we teach about Jesus, we should make it clear that the Law of karma is bad for people. The bad news is that they can't escape their bad karma. But the good news is that God's love is *for* the world, to save it. It is man's own insistence on not receiving God's love that makes it exclusive. Man excludes himself. When that happens, the Law of karma condemns him to an uncertain future. The next chapter will detail how to tell the message so that it comes across in a way that reveals and confirms what people already know in their hearts, not in a way that condemns them.

* * * * * * * *

5. Centering our message around doctrine and ritual.

I spent my whole life in Asia combatting the viruses of sectarian bias and denom-inational superiority. These are the strongest influences for dividing the church. For example, one denomination teaches its own interpretation of baptism, the Lord's Supper, and church government. Meanwhile, other Christians are teaching different interpretations of the Bible. Pure, unadulterated communities of believers have been split into small factions, because they were introduced to differing doctrines and rituals, each proclaimed as the Truth.

Other doctrines and rituals taught by Christians are simply Old Testament cultural and social structures, yet they are proclaimed as God's exclusive way for all cultures, societies, and eras. The principle of tithing is a good example. I remember sitting in a Lahu village, talking with a Red Lahu shaman about Jesus Christ. He became so excited about the gospel story and about God's love that he exclaimed before everyone sitting in the house that he could not wait any longer; he had to make this decision about becoming a Christian. But then he said he had to figure out his finances and see how much money he had.

"You don't need money to become a Christian," I said.

"But I must pay the tax when I become a Christian," he said.

"There's no tax," I said.

"Oh yes," he replied. "Everybody has to pay ten percent."

Our teaching on the tithe for this man had become a barrier to his salvation. Receiving salvation was easy, but maintaining his faith in a Christian church context was a serious difficulty to him. Yet a quick check in the concordance shows that nearly all references to tithing are in the Old Testament. Those few in the New Testament occur when Jesus condemns the Pharisees, or when the writer of Hebrews quotes the Old Testament scriptures in order to tell about Abraham. But Love stresses giving from a willing heart, not from adherence to culturally bound legalism.

Missionary strategists and researchers have long known that the greatest barrier to receiving the truth, regardless of who speaks it, is culture. Receiving and following Truth often has dire consequences in light of a person's traditions and culture. Jesus showed this when He spoke about those who would be persecuted for His name's sake, and when He taught about those who would leave father or mother, sister or brother for Him: "He who loves father or mother more than Me is not worthy of Me; And he who loves son or daughter more than Me is not worthy of Me; And he who does not take his cross and follow after Me is not worthy of Me." [11] All of these can be barriers: father or mother, son or daughter, having to bear a "cross." What Jesus is saying is, "Have love to the point that you will lay down your life freely."

Still, it is not easy for people to follow Truth if it demands moral or ethical judgments that require radical changes in their social behaviors. The human heart is easily deceived about its own true motives and biases. A person may want to have sexual license or to be identified with the crowd so much that he is not willing to pursue a more honorable ethic than the crowd is willing to accept.

People naturally love their own culture. Its religious forms supply the spiritual comfort they feel they need. They believe they are righteous when they follow these forms. Even when people perceive that the rituals and ceremonies of their culture are more lifestyle than religion, these customs may be vitally important to them. We should be sensitive to their needs and should respect their customs. (See appendix A, chapter 14.)

Jesus respected people from different cultural backgrounds. He showed mercy with unquestioning love and acceptance to those shunned by His culture and society. He touched the leper. He said of the Roman captain, "I have not seen so great a faith, no not in Israel." [12] To the Syrophoenician woman, whose heritage was that of the

Philistines, He showed mercy. He required of them no ritual, no act of purification, no specific form of worship, no searching and memorization of the Torah, no keeping of the Sabbath. To Jesus, no doctrines or rituals could take the place of a pure, contrite heart. That's what He complimented: "Blessed are the pure in heart."[13]

Barriers can rise when we try to impose our culture on another person. Our church forms, culturally based, are not meant for everyone. The eternal Truth and its accompanying mercy, justice, and caring never change, but the cultural forms in which Truth is expressed are in constant flux. It is wrong to force upon present cultures our interpretation of ancient forms followed in biblical culture, and it is wrong to use these forms as the test of devotion to God. These ancient forms no longer convey God's love to the people of today.

We have also created a program-oriented Western church and have communicated that people must take part in those programs in order to be strong, solid Christians. Yet this becomes a barrier to many people. The result is that we have cut off potentially receptive people. Programs can be a real work of the Holy Spirit to meet the needs of families or to evangelize, but we must be careful to make sure these programs are not perceived as commandments which every Christian must obey. Secular man fears that our programs are mandates that he must accept, and he feels he can't join the program. I don't know the solution to this. But I do know we need to present the gospel in such a way that all people can come to Jesus without having to cross this barrier.

Jesus said, "I will build my church."[14] What he is saying is that the love He has shown, when embraced, will bring people together. Is it possible for the Holy Spirit to move in such a way that within each community's cultural variances and necessities, people can receive Jesus exactly where they are and be completely accepted when they simply make a full confession of faith? What can we do to create such a world church?

* * * * * * * *

6. Approaching a person by first addressing his sin.

If we approach a person by pointing out or condemning his sin, we fall into a pit we can't crawl out of, because there's no end to the sin we could find. But if we come simply teaching Jesus, then we communicate the positive value of love. When a person *perceives* God's love, his sins come into sharp contrast to God's virtues. If he *receives* God's love, he experiences a cleansed heart, and new spirit within him. He has God as his standard, his Mark, and he has, as well, a second chance at life. The Holy Spirit will convict his spirit of his sin. [15]

In the story of the tribal village, notice that with all the degradation that was there, what we took in with us and what we focused on was not a condemnation of their actions, but the message that they can be redeemed. If we had gone in condemning their evil behavior — planting, selling, and smoking opium, letting their children smoke it, selling their daughters into prostitution — they would have driven us out of the village before we had said another word. Not that such condemnation wouldn't have been true. But it's not the starting point.

Our starting point is telling the villagers of the love of God and the beauty of His Holy Spirit. So instead of their hearts hardening against the message, their hearts become open and pliable to the good news. If they then receive the message of Jesus Christ, welcome Him into their lives, and accept the Holy Spirit in place of their evil spirits, then the Holy Spirit will create a deep shame in them. They will no longer sell their children or enslave them to opium addiction. The Holy Spirit will lead them gently into a new way of living. They themselves will choose to change their sinful behavior.

Evidence of this is not hard to find. If we drive into a primarily Christian village after what we have seen in the animistic one, the difference is startling. There are latrines and water pipes. Clean children and young unmarried girls greet us with smiles. The opium houses are gone, and so are the tourists coming to smoke it. A rustic wood and bamboo church house crowns the highest place in the village. The leaders are making efforts to get the children educated. Fear of the spirits has given way to smiles and laughter.

We do not want to condone sin. But we want to get away from condemnation in our message. Sin is a burden that man cannot bear, and God is tender and non-condemning when we miss the Mark. The scriptures show us that Jesus and Paul did not focus on sin or on the condemnation of sinners. Instead, they concentrated on the positive: God's power to redeem and reconcile and set men free by the Law of the Spirit of life in Christ.

For example, Jesus told the story of the good Samaritan. We see sin in this story, but Jesus did not point it out. Instead, He pointed out the kind act. This is typical of the Scriptures, which show us positive acts, then show that there were those who didn't receive them. The beautiful fact that the Scriptures accentuate is that Jesus died for the sins of the whole world. The sting of death is sin. The power of sin is the Law. But now death is swallowed up in victory. [16]

**We do not want to condone sin.
But we want to get away from condemnation in our message.**

What Jesus does is restore the Mark, all that makes humanity beautiful and harmonious: the love that is seen in the cross. Jesus enables people to live with their frailties and mistakes, because His blood has cleansed them and set them on the upward path. Now, instead of trying to do away with the concept of sin, people can admit their inability to bear the burden of sin, and allow Jesus to do away with condemnation.

* * * * * * *

7. Communicating with confusing words.

We can't be locked into Christianese if we want to communicate with non-believers or with those who have become dis-enchanted with the church. On one side of the coin, we must be aware that New Age philosophy uses many
of the same words we use, but with a different definition or slant. On the other side of the coin, many of our words turn off hearers and get in the way of the message.

For example, the Christian says to the Buddhist, "God loves you," believing that this is good news. But for those who dismiss God as a reality, this means nothing. "There is no proof for believing that there is a God," they might respond (although characteristically, Thai Buddhists would not argue, they would simply listen stoically, feeling nothing).

In addition, one Thai teacher told me, "Love is the problem of mankind and the source of his suffering." Love, to Buddhists, is the cause of all sin, because they equate the word "love" with "desire," a desire like that which Eve had for the forbidden fruit. A cardinal foundation in Buddhist philosophy is that "all is suffering." The cause of suffering is desire and attachment. Love is the strongest word they can use for expressing attachment. In other words, you love someone, they die, you suffer. Therefore, in their thinking, no love, no suffering, no pain.

Add to this the fact that in Buddhism, "you" do not exist. "Buddhism forgoes. . .the theories of a permanent individual soul." [17]
So in this setting, to say, "God loves you" is not an effective way to begin communicating the message of Jesus Christ. If we say, "God loves you," all the Buddhist hears is, "Nothing real causes suffering to something that does not exist."

Many people in Western societies today are drawn to Eastern philosophies and may speak with their terminology. When they say, "All is God," or "God is everything," can we use their non-traditional language to show that all of creation is nothing but the word of God in manifest form? That God upholds all things by the word of His power? That we are not God, but His creation, sustained by His love? They may use the word "redeemer," not referring to Jesus Christ, or as we have seen, talk about christ, not meaning Jesus. Can we communicate to the New Age believer, in his terminology, the Truth that he knows he knows?

There's also the issue of politically correct language. This is important to many people. Although this book has consistently used the terms "man" and "mankind" as inclusive of both genders, when we talk to others, we should be sensitive of their "hot buttons." Of course, the list of words that might offend people could go on and on. For example, some people might hate the word "Father," because they've had bad experiences with their own father. Every word has the potential to offend *someone*. So it's impossible to identify or discuss them all. This is why it's important to listen to people as you dialogue, and then be sensitive as you speak. When you sense that someone has a lot of "hot buttons," you might try to circumvent those words in your own vocabulary. Here are a few that have proved to be touchy. You may know others. Depending upon how the conversation is flowing, and to whom you are speaking, you can give an explanation of the word. Any of the following could be stated in different ways that conform to the gospel message:

Sin/Sinner:	You might call sin "missing the Mark."
Repentance:	When God changes your mind, your purposes, and your life.
Salvation:	When God brings you into a personal, living relationship with Him.
Born-again:	When God gives you a whole new spirit and recreates your very heart and image, and gives you power to live.
Gospel:	The greatest message you will ever hear: "God loves you."
God's Son:	God imaging Himself in the form of man under Law to fulfill Law for all men.. (God is invisible. God's Son is simply God manifesting Himself in human form that we may see and understand His heart.)

Even the word "Jesus" can be a turn-off if you bring Him up too soon. It might be helpful to encourage the person to "plug into the person God has made you to be" and to emphasize that "You'll find a beauty in Jesus Christ that you'll never find anywhere else."

* * * * * * *

We've considered a few barriers built by the post-modern culture in which we now live. [18] We've also considered barriers that we ourselves often inadvertently set up. Some of these barriers are too high. If you try to tackle them, you will lose the person you're talking to. So go around those barriers. Allow the person to dismantle the barrier themselves by coming to the love of Jesus. That's when these barriers begin to fall.

> **Allow the person to dismantle the barrier themselves
> by coming to the love of Jesus.
> That's when these barriers begin to fall.**

1. 1 Corinthians 2:2
2. John 16:13
3. Matthew 7:13, 14
4. Matthew 22:13
5. John 8:24
6. Madeleine L'Engle, <u>Walking on Water</u> (Wheaton: Shaw, 1980) 122.
7. Anna Leonowens, <u>The English Governess in the Siamese Court</u> (Oxford: Oxford UP, 1988) 53.
8. Acts 17:22, 23
9. This doesn't mean we can't stand against Satan and his wiles. Most Christian efforts to resist the evil spirits which bind a nation are excellent efforts and can be done without offending.
10. Matthew 13:15
11. Matthew 10:37, 38
12. Matthew 8:10
13. Matthew 16:18
14. John 16:8
15. 1 Corinthians 15:54-56
16. Dr. Luan Siryapong, <u>Buddhism in the Light of Modern Scientific Ideas</u> (Bangkok: Mahamagutrad UP, 1954) 6, 7.
17. You can read more about the mind-set of our post-modern culture in books like <u>The Emerging Church</u> by Dan Kimball.

Interlude

Discovering an Unknown God

Long ago on the rocky isle of Crete, there lived a poet named Epimenides. He was well-respected and was considered to be quite wise. One day, Epimenides received a visit from Nicias, one of the many esteemed philosophers of Athens, a city widely known for its many gods. Epimenides had heard that Athens was full of idols, for it was a common saying that there were more idols in Athens than in all the rest of Greece. But Epimenides had also heard that Athens was full of something else: a deadly plague.

In fact it was this plague that had motivated the leaders of Athens to send Nicius to Crete to beg advice from Epimenides. The Athenians had sacrificed to every god in the city, but to no avail. The plague still surged, threatening to destroy the entire population. The leaders wondered if perhaps there was another god, one whom they had overlooked, who might regard their sacrifices with favor and save them from the ravages of the plague.

Epimenides accompanied Nicius back to Athens where he informed the leaders that he agreed with them: There was indeed another god, one whose name neither he nor the Athenians knew. The problem was that since they did not know this god, they did not know what sacrifice would please him. So Epimenides came up with a plan. He asked that a flock of sheep, some black and some white, be brought to Mars Hill early the next morning. At dawn on the following day, shepherds, sheep, and city leaders made their way to Mars Hill. When they had all gathered, Epimenides instructed the shepherds to let their flock wander over the hill, taking notice of any that lay down. Normally, none would lay down, because at that time of day they would all be hungry. But as the people watched, one sheep lay down. Then another. And another. Epimenides told the people to build an altar where each sheep lay and then sacrifice that sheep on the altar, for each reclining sheep was a sign that the unknown god had chosen that one as a sacrifice to himself.

Many sheep were sacrificed that day to a god whose name the people did not know. By the end of the week, the plague had subsided, and the Athenians were recovering. In gratitude, the people lay flowers at the altars and inscribed the structures with the words TO AN UNKNOWN GOD.

Whether or not this legend is true, it is important to note that the Athenians perceived that the plague had been imposed upon them because of their sin. To appease the god, the sacrifice would have to be one that the god chose. As they followed Epimenides' plan, they saw that the god pointed out what the sacrifice was to be, and when they offered the sacrifice, the plague was lifted.

William Barclay, "The Acts of the Apostles," The Daily Study Bible, rev. ed. (Edinburgh: Saint Andrews) 130.

Don Richardson. Eternity in Their Hearts, (Ventura, CA: Regal, 1981) 14-20.

CHAPTER FIFTEEN

Telling What You Know You Know

Generations Later, On Mars Hill

> *Now while Paul waited for them at Athens, his spirit was provoked within him when he saw that the city was given over to idols. Therefore he reasoned in the synagogue with the Jews and with the Gentile worshipers, and in the marketplace daily. . . . Then Paul stood in the midst of the Areopagus and said, "Men of Athens, I perceive that in all things you are very religious; for as I was passing through and considering the objects of your worship, I even found an altar with this inscription: TO THE UNKNOWN GOD. Therefore, the One whom you worship without knowing, Him I proclaim to you. . . ."*
>
> Acts 17:16, 17, 22, 23, NKJV

At the time Paul spoke at the Areopagus (also known as Mars Hill), the Athenians knew well the background history of the Unknown God. Their ancestors had listened gladly to Epimenides. Now here before them was another wise man from the Unknown God. This God, with his great concern for their life and happiness, had left such a mark upon them that their hearts were open to learn all that he might say to them.

Paul's message was simple, but profound. He used the Athenians' own altar of worship as a common denominator and quoted their own philosophers. He knew that they viewed *ignorance* as sin, considering it the evil of all evils. So he spoke of God's patience and tolerance toward their ignorance. Paul was aware that they believed in a judgment and a Hades that had many compartments. So he blended this into his presentation, along with other facets of God's love for the world, His impartiality to all people, and His presence with all people. Let's hear Paul speak to what he knew they knew:

> "This Unknown God is the Maker of heaven and earth and has created all men, not just the Athenians," said Paul. "This God is close. We are His offspring, His sons. We bear His image. In the past, you were ignorant of God, and He overlooked your ignorance. But God will no longer wink at your ignorance. He now commands all people to repent, change their minds, change their ways.
>
> "You all believe in Hades. You believe that you must receive punishment for the evil you've done. But God has appointed a day when He will judge the world rightly and justly. For He has given us evidence in His Son whom He raised from the dead." [1]

Notice that we hear the Truth of *all* of Paul's points from the Athenians' point of view. So when Paul speaks of the resurrection from the dead, he implies that the Law of karma has been broken. That's why his listeners got so excited. To them, the Law of karma represented that they had to be reincarnated. But they could see what Paul was alluding to: Jesus was the provided sheep that had already been sacrificed. The Unknown God had chosen and provided the sacrifice Himself. Now death in Hades would reign no more, for God had raised the sacrifice from the dead. The plague of sin and death had been conquered.

What most amazed the Athenians was Paul's teaching about resurrection as opposed to the reincarnation and rebirth advocated by their philosophies. By the time Paul concluded, many wanted to hear more about this resurrection from the dead. Paul's presentation had been dynamic. It had opened their hearts.

For years I prayed for a one-time Mars Hill presentation like the one Paul made to the men of Athens: a brief, dynamic witness that would leave people with the knowledge that they cannot ignore Jesus. One day I prayed about this for quite some time. Then at last I saw it: Paul's apologetic in Acts 17, his argument in defense of God and His plan. At the time, I was driving, and I got so excited I had to pull to the side of the road so I could cheer and thank God.

I saw that what Paul did *not* say on Mars Hill is just as significant as what he did say. Paul was fully aware of the Athenians' presuppositions, so he began with their accepted position. He did not condemn or curse their idols, and he did not debate their varied philosophical viewpoints. Instead, he capitalized on common ground.

In the previous chapters, I described the self-verification of Jesus as the Christ. Over and over again, I pointed out the common ground we have with people today and stressed the need to always glorify God. Now let's take a last, close look at how we can use what we have learned and plug into the same concept Paul used, not criticizing, but starting with a common denominator.

Becoming a Witness

We cannot and should not stay silent. God's great love grips our lives, so from the rising to the setting of the sun, our desire is for the world to know His name. Our entire effort must be to witness Christ, to help others see so that they can make a valid decision. Jesus gave us the way to reach the world. He handed it to us. In effect, he told us that the way the world is wired, if we proclaim the message and live the love, they will get it.

When you start a conversation with someone, speak at first only of what both of you can agree on. If you tell a person what you think he believes, you have lost him. But if you speak what you both know to be True in a universal sense, you remain in agreement, and the conversation continues.

If what we say does not sound like the Truth to a person, that person will dismiss it.

The first step in touching the secular world is to bring them to what they know: that the kind of love seen in the cross fulfills all the requirements of the Law. That kind of love reveals the personal nature of God and the beauty of His reign in the human heart. Truth is in everyone. You don't have to teach it, you just tap into it. That's what Paul did. He tapped into the Athenians' belief in the Unknown God. So talk only about the universal Truth that the person knows to be true instead of disagreeing with his belief system. For where does Truth find itself confirmed? Only in the hearer's heart. The listener is the one who confirms or denies. We might as well concede that if what we say to a person does not sound like the Truth to him, he will dismiss it.

For example, if I am addressing the naturalist, atheist, or deist, I try to speak to him from his perspective. I rely on the Spirit of Truth to verify to his spirit that what I am saying is true. If I give up the Spirit of Truth as grounds of proof and debate him in the physical realm, relying on human proof, I am in a no-win situation. So I do not try to prove the Bible.

I also allow him to hold his conclusions about how our world came into existence. Such a concession may grind the nerves of some Christians, but the argument for Jesus as the manifest revelation of God's love for the world is best made by letting the atheist's theories stand as peripheral issues. Why? Because his theories lead us to a common denominator, a belief both of us hold: We exist in a realm of Law. For instance, the naturalist, atheist, or deist grants that natural Law, the cause and effect principle, was at work on cosmic elements to predetermine the effect of the "Big Bang." He acknowledges that Law kept the elements from continuing in a state of chaos and produced our world with its interdependence of all living and non-living things, beautiful in its symmetry and design.

So for the atheist, I first talk about Law, not about Jesus or even God. The atheist would have to agree that evolution has resulted in the highest form that has ever evolved: thinking man. And the highest level that man can think of is a Supreme Being of infinite love. This is exactly what the natural Law that governs evolution gives witness to: the love of a Supreme Being who has given this natural Law to control the evolutionary process. This idea is a product of evolution. It is a living fact that the evolutionist must assent to. So it makes a complete circle. If we start with Law, it brings us to God and His love. If we start with God and His love, it brings us to Law, then back to God again.

Now if a Supreme Being of infinite love is the highest thought of man, then God has to love at least as deeply as the greatest human love, which is self-sacrificial. So God must be personal, because love is personal. God has to be the essence and meaning of a life of peace and love. How could we know this unless God had placed within us this knowledge of Himself?

Say to a person only what is true to him.

I take a similar path when I talk to a Buddhist. I do not ask him to transfer his belief from Buddha to Christ in the sense of asking him to exchange one teacher for another. Instead, I ask him simply to confirm the faith that already resides within him: the knowledge that people cannot keep the Law; only God can keep the Law, which He did, as man in Jesus. All I do is take the love of Jesus into the Buddhist's culture and show how Jesus' love flows through his philosophy.

I do much the same when talking to someone who holds the New Age philosophy. I don't start by correcting him; I go with his terms. We can both talk about the "Supreme Source" or the "Divine Essence." He doesn't have to say "God." We can also agree on the words "redeemer" and "forgiver" and man's need for both. Or we might discuss the common christ in every person, or the Law of karma. Then I can springboard from the moral Law to show how it must be fulfilled.

In any case, I say nothing about church. The church is the application of love, the fellowship that love seeks. So churches will form naturally within a specific culture's customs. This is important to remember when you talk to those who have grown disenchanted with the church and have stopped attending. In the United States, the number of unchurched people has increased 92% in the last thirteen years, and 54% of those (over 40 million people) consider themselves to be Christian. Surprisingly, around 10 million of the unchurched adult Christians consider themselves born again. [2] If I talk about church to the disenchanted, I bring in a negative. So I don't bring it up, because I don't want them to walk away without hearing the message of God's love. I believe that if they embrace Jesus once again, He will build them into His church.

Love seeks community. So my goal is to communicate God's love through Jesus in a way that all people can see it in its simple beauty. People still may not want to darken the doors of a church building. But at least I know that if they believe in Jesus, they are the church and will naturally seek community. Once people believe in Jesus and are growing in Him, He'll bring them along, because He is Love.

The Promise for You

I have chosen not to present a methodology. [3] My hope is that you can hear the promise Jesus has given you. He will guide you. When Jesus sent the first believers out, He gave them only one thing: the Holy Spirit of Truth to bear witness to Him. When they wondered, "What do we say? How do we act?" His words must have echoed in their hearts: "Love one another as I have loved you." "Feed my sheep." "No one takes my life. I freely lay it down." "I came not to be served, but to serve." "The Son of Man has come to seek and save that which was lost." Jesus did not give them a seven-step presentation of the message. Instead, he said, "Take no thought about what to say, for if your heart is filled with the Spirit, you'll know what to say." "Rest assured that they *will* persecute you, even in the religious synagogues." But "I will be with you always, even to the end of the world." [4]

What is important here is that you now know you are not judging or criticizing people. You understand that people cannot see God's love when they approach Him through Law. Unless they understand Jesus, they cannot perceive the love and grace of a living God who has a purpose and destiny for their lives. So this should set you at ease in your discussion with them. It is God who converts the heart. It is yours to present the message as clearly and reasonably as you can.

We grow in this skill from day to day. The only real way to learn to witness is to do it. Sometimes you'll get stuck, as sometimes I do. You'll never finish all conversations thinking you did a great job. You may realize you said an inappropriate word or went a direction that ended the conversation. This still happens to me, so don't feel disheartened. Some people can't receive it. Go to someone else. You've got to be happy with what you can do at that moment. Just know that a verbal witness is necessary. If you don't preach Jesus, they'll never understand.

Paul wrote that we have not been given a spirit of fear. So when you are trying to witness Jesus, but don't know what to do, remember Acts 4. The believers prayed and praised God for His power. Then they were filled with the Spirit and spoke boldly. They went everywhere teaching. This was the power of the Spirit of witness in the first century church. They had no New Testament. Every disciple became a teacher, preacher, and philosopher, because he had to address the philosophical teachings of his day. Every Christian home became a cell group. Their message was not the church, not the ceremonial rituals, not the forms, not the doctrines. Their message was Truth.

When we say Truth, we simply say Jesus and all He embodied. You can trust Truth, because Truth is not what, but Who. He is:

> the image of God in you
>> the fulfillment of the law for you
>>> the God who died for you.

Truth is not what, but Who.

He is:
    your Hope
        your Faith
            your Light
                your Way
                    your Love
                        your Life.

He is the Truth you know you know.
And the Truth verifies Himself.
He is just that way.

A free, down-loadable study guide is available online for those who want to use this book as a course of study. You can find it at: www.TheTruthYouKnowYouKnow.com

---

1. Paraphrase, Acts 17:24, 27, 30-31.

2. George Barna, "Number of Unchurched Adults Has Nearly Doubled Since 1991" Barna Research Online (4 May 2004), 8 July 2004 < www.barna.org/FlexPage.aspx?Page=BarnaUpdate&BarnaUpdateID=163>.

3. For those who want to see an example of how I witness through dialogue, see the appendix.

4. John 13:34, John 21:17, John 10:18, Matthew 20:28, Luke 19:10, Luke 12:11, 12, Luke 21:12, Matthew 28:20

Appendix A

Further Reference Material

The following reference material provides more extensive information on the topics covered in this book. Each reference is categorized under the chapter heading for which it provides additional insight.

Chapter 2: Two Dimensions of Truth

Plato and Aristotle

Plato organized the idealism of Socrates into a systematic philosophy. In his theory of Ideas, Plato regarded objects of the real world as shadows of eternal Forms or Ideas. He taught that only these changeless, eternal Forms can be the object of true knowledge; the perception of their shadows (the real world that is heard, seen, and felt) is merely opinion. The goal of the philosopher, he said, is to know the eternal Forms and to instruct others in that knowledge.

Microsoft® Encarta® 98 Encyclopedia. © 1993-1997 Microsoft Corporation, s.v. "Greek Philosophy."

Chapter 5: The Common Denominator

Natural Law

In philosophy of science, a universal statement that describes and/or explains the course of natural events (e.g., Newton's laws of motion); in jurisprudence and political philosophy, a system of right or justice common to all humankind and derived from nature rather than from the rules of society, or positive law.

This concept can be traced back to Aristotle, who held that what was "just by nature" was not always the same as what was "just by law." In one form or another, the existence of natural law was asserted by the Stoics (see Stoicism), Cicero, the Roman jurists, St. Paul, St. Augustine, Gratian, Thomas Aquinas, John Duns Scotus, William of Ockham, and Francisco Suarez. In the modern period, Hugo Grotius and Thomas Hobbes constructed a system of natural law by deduction from a "state of nature" followed by a social contract. John Locke described the state of nature as a state of society based on natural law. J. J. Rousseau postulated a savage who was virtuous in isolation and actuated by self-preservation and compassion. The Declaration of Independence refers only briefly to "the Laws of Nature" before citing equality and other "unalienable" rights as "self-evident." The French Declaration of the Rights of Man and of the Citizen asserts liberty, property, security, and resistance to oppression as "imprescriptible natural rights."

Encyclopædia Britannica Inc., Britannica Concise CD Rom, 2002, s.v. "Natural Law"

Declaration of Independence: "...and to assume among the powers of the earth, the separate and equal station to which the Laws of Nature and Nature's God entitle them....We hold these truths to be self-evident, that all men are created equal, that they are endowed by their Creator with certain unalienable Rights..."

Enclyclopædia Britannica 2005 Ultimate Reference Suite CD-Rom, Version: 2005.00, s.v. "Declaration of Independence," from the text of the "Declaration of Independence (1776) In Congress, July 4, 1776."

Karl Marx: "It is absolutely impossible to transcend the laws of nature. What can change in historically different circumstances is only the form in which these laws expose themselves."
From Letter to Dr. Kugelmann 11 July 1868 (published in <u>Karl Marx, Frederick Engles:</u> <u>Collected Works</u>, trans. Richard Dixon et. al, Vol. 38, 1992).

Philo on Universal law

Philo Judaeus lived in Alexandria from 20BC to 50AD, contemporary with the Apostle Paul. A theologian and a philosopher, Philo wrote for the Greeks, attempting to bring them to the Jewish faith. To win the pagan (Greek) world to God, Philo bases his argument on the Law of Nature, which is the same argument Paul used to win Jews and Gentiles to Christ. The common denominator that Greeks, Jews, and Romans accepted was law. Philo also used law to establish a moral and ethical code by which city states and the nations could govern and the world community could be at peace. - KR

"But since every city in which laws are properly established, has a regular constitution, it became necessary for this citizen of the world to adopt the same constitution as that which prevailed in the universal world. And this constitution is the right reason of nature, which in more appropriate language is denominated law, being a divine arrangement in accordance with which everything suitable and appropriate is assigned to every individual. But of this city and constitution there must have been some citizens before man, who might be justly called citizens of a mighty city, having received the greatest imaginable circumference to dwell in; and having been enrolled in the largest and most perfect commonwealth."

Philo Judaeus. <u>The Works of Philo</u>. (Oak Harbor, WA: Logos Research Systems, 1997).

The Law of Karma (Kamma)

"Kamma (Karma) means action, doing work, business; and the Law of Kamma may be described as the Law of Cause and effect. Very briefly stated it is this: everything that happens does so only by reason of some earlier cause, so does the result. Everything is the effect of some cause and is itself the cause of some other effect. This law, the Buddha declares, holds true in every department of the universe. As far as a man is concerned, this is the law that affects his happiness or sorrow. It has no origin in time; it is not a 'command', therefore it cannot be broken. Thus in Buddhism, there is no such thing as a sin as a violation of God's 'command'.

"No one can, however, disregard the law of karma without paying the penalty. It cannot be altered by beseeching, by self-torture, or by offerings. No God can interfere with it. Gone therefore is the need for prayers, ceremonies and rights, and the priesthood required for their celebration."

Dr. G. P. Malalasekera, <u>Buddhism in Ceylon</u>   (Colombo: The Ceylon Tourist Board, n.d.), page 9

Chapter 6   The Wrath of the Law

"Wrath of God" Scriptures in the New Testament

The Greek word 'orge,' (wrath) occurs four times in the phrase "the wrath of God": John 3:36; Rom. 1:18; Eph. 5:6; Col. 3:6. At times its use describes judgment. But, the New Testament message is not the "impassionate wrath" and "vengeance" that Greeks and Romans perceived in their gods or that Jews ascribed to God in the Old Testament. Paul explained that it is the Law that brings wrath. The Pagan world never perceived that the "Holy, just, and good" Law was the instrument of wrath to them, instead of God being wrath. Rather, the Law made sin known and became the "law of sin and death," the instrument for condemnation of sin. "The Law brings wrath." Under Law, wrath is inescapable. -KR

"He who believes in the Son has eternal life; but he who does not obey the Son shall not see life, but the wrath of God abides on him" (John 3:36). This passage is not a condemnation, but a promise of life to be received. If one receives God's love and grace, one receives God's gift of life. If one wills freely to remain under the Law (of one's own action or karma) and receive the effect of sin, then one's karma of darkness is an eternal separation from God, His love, and His life. It is a free choice one makes: God's grace or one's own karma. -KR

In the three scriptures below, Paul is talking to men under Law. The Law is the wrath of God:

> "For the wrath of God is revealed from heaven against all ungodliness and unrighteousness of men, who suppress the truth in unrighteousness, because that which is known about God is evident within them; for God made it evident to them. For since the creation of the world His invisible attributes, His eternal power and divine nature, have been clearly seen, being understood through what has been made, so that they are without excuse." Romans 1:18-20

> "Let no one deceive you with empty words, for because of these things the wrath of God comes upon the sons of disobedience."
> Ephesians 5:6

> "Therefore consider the members of your earthly body as dead to immorality, impurity, passion, evil desire, and greed, which amounts to idolatry. For it is on account of these things that the wrath of God will come." Colossians 3:6

Finally, I quote the following passages to help show how God remains righteous and just when He allows the Law's cause and effect principle to run its course to those who choose their own righteousness under Law. But always, His loving grace as a gift is available to anyone who gives up his own self for God's righteous Self. -KR

"For God has not destined us for wrath, but for obtaining salvation through our Lord Jesus Christ, who died for us, that whether we are awake or asleep, we may live together with Him."
1 Thessalonians 5:9

"But if our unrighteousness demonstrates the righteousness of God, what shall we say? The God who inflicts wrath is not unrighteous, is He? (I am speaking in human terms.) May it never be! For otherwise how will God judge the world?"   Romans 3:5

Chapter 10   Christ Unrealized and Christ Realized

The Previousness of Christ

"God is at work in all nations. Those who are very enthusiastic for evangelistic work among rural villages often claim that they were the 'first people' to bring the gospel to this particular village. They do not realize that even before they entered and proclaimed the word of God to the particular community or village, God was at work within the community and his presence was there as the 'previousness of Christ'...the work of God through the Holy Spirit."

"The Success Story of Shanthi," by W.S. Milton Jeganathan from <u>Transformation, An International Dialogue on Mission and Ethics</u>, p.49 Vol 21 No 1 January 2004

The article above makes a good point: God is at work in all people even before they are "reached." God is at work in every culture, leaving each culture with a witness of Himself through the christ in them, although they do not know the gospel of Jesus until it is proclaimed. We cannot do away with the power of the proclamation. -KR

Interiority of Faith

"...God's presence to the human self is more interior and secret than the human self's own interiority and secretness to itself. And more idiosyncratic — for God made this very idiosyncratic territory and secretness, that is, the 'I.' According to Hopkins, this is the greatest and principal thing that God made, the centre of each human being and the ultimate focus of exterior creation, of the cosmos. An Indian Jesuit ascetical theologian, Anthony De Mello, writing out of an intimate acquaintanceship both with Ignatius' Spiritual Exercises and with Eastern religious sensibility, puts it this way (49): 'For you there is no reality that is closer to God than yourself. St. Augustine would therefore rightly insist that we must restore man to himself so that he can make of himself a stepping stone to God.'"

Walter J. Ong, <u>Hopkins, the Self, and God</u> (Univ. of Toronto Press, 1986) 144.

Dhamma

"Finally we come to the most important term of all, which is, God the Saviour. We even define 'God' further as the World Saviour, who will save the world from being in an undesirable state....All in all we can see that it is 'God' who saves this world, by God we must mean an impersonal God. If God is a personal God who acts and appears like human beings, capable of getting angry and so forth, then we cannot accept Him....to say that Truth is God is quite correct, because Truth is nothing personal...If we now substitute the word Dhamma for God, then there can be no misunderstanding, for God is Truth, Truth is God, and always so, because it means an impersonal God, which is Dhamma....It has the power to protect or save the world, if men will help make it possible...."

"In terms of sense or value, it (Dhamma) becomes Religion which will bind men to Nirvana or God. ...in terms of... the supernatural we would have to say that Dhamma is God in every sense of the word."

Venerable Buddhadasa Bhikkhu, <u>Dhamma-The World Savior</u>, The Friend Mission Inter religious Literature Series #1 (Bangkok: Friend Muslim Mission, 1965) 14-18.

Chapter 11   The Equation of Faith

Faith of Christ

"Just as one speaks of "Christ-faith" and means by it not the faith by which Christ believes but the faith by which he is believed in, so one speaks of the righteousness of God and means not that righteousness by which God is righteous. Both are ours. But they are called God's and Christ's righteousness and faith, because they are given to us by his bounty."

Martin Luther, "Lectures on Romans," <u>The Library of Christian Classics</u>, Ichthus Edition, trans, ed Wilhelm Pauck (Philadelphia: Westminster, 1961) 109.

Chapter 13:   Cultural Barriers

On Buddhist teaching against the use of scripture or theory or tradition as authoritative in establishing truth:

"On one occasion the Enlightened One came to the village of Kesaputta where lived certain tribesmen known as the Kalamas. They knew the Buddha to be a renowned spiritual teacher and addressed him as follows:

> There are some monks and Brahmins, Venerable Sir, who visit Kessaputta. They illustrate and illuminate only their own doctrines; the doctrines of others they despise, revile and pull to pieces. Venerable Sir, there is doubt, there is uncertainty, in us concerning them. Which of these reverend monks and Brahmins spoke the truth and which falsehood?

"To this the Buddha replied:

> It is proper for you, Kalamas, to doubt; to be uncertain. Uncertainty has arisen in you, about what is doubtful. Come, Kalamas. Do not go upon an authoritative tradition; nor upon what has been acquired by repeated hearing; nor upon rumour; nor upon what is in a scripture; nor upon speculative metaphysical theories, reasons and arguments; nor upon a point of view; nor upon specious reasoning; nor upon accepting a statement as true because it agrees with a theory that one is already convinced of; nor upon another's seeming ability; nor upon the consideration 'Our teacher says thus and so'. Kalamas, when you yourselves know: 'These things are bad; these things are blamable; these things are censured by the wise; undertaken and observed, these things lead to harm and ill, abandon them.' (Anguitara-Nikaya 1, 189)"

Chom Sookparimat, <u>Buddhism: The Religion in Thailand</u> (Bangkok:

World Fellowship of Buddhists Regional Centre of Thailand, c/o Buddhist Association of Thailand) 6, 7.

Chapter 14: Barriers WE Build

On the Bible

"The true heart goes to the blessed Book, not as an idolater, but as a disciple; not to worship the Book, but to learn the will of him who made the Book and who has made his spirit to understand the Book."

George MacDonald, <u>God's Word to His Children</u> (New York; Funk and Wagnalls, 1887) 113.

Attending a Buddhist Funeral

Missionaries often struggle with knowing what they can do and how far they can go in touching the lives of people in other religions. One way we settled this was by going to Buddhist funerals for Thai friends. What we would call "visitation" took place in a special area of a temple compound. The body lay in front in a coffin surrounded by flowers. A priest sat on one side, chanting prayers. Incense was burning. In front of the coffin, there was an area for paying respect to the deceased. Here a visitors would sit on the floor, legs folded to the side, and "wai" (make the traditional Thai gesture of respect by pressing his hands together, resting the thumbs on the nose, fingers extended up toward the forehead). Then he would bow until his elbows touched the ground. After that, he would light a joss stick (incense stick) and place it in a receptacle in front of the coffin. This paid respect to the dead. Next the mourner would turn and also pay respect to the Buddha image by bowing and "wai-ing" three times.

We believed that the two actions of respect were distinct and could be separated. One action was paying honor to the deceased. The other was paying religious homage in a Buddhist ritual. So, we attended these gatherings to honor the one who had died. We bowed before the coffin, "wai-ed", and lit a joss stick. However, we did not bow or give respect directly to the Buddha image.

Thai people greatly appreciated our coming and giving respect to their friend or family member. They were not offended when we did not show homage to the Buddha. So attending these ceremonies became a way for us to move with the Thais in their culture, respecting the rites that held great meaning and reverence to them, yet without practicing their religion. -KR

Appendix B

An Example of Witnessing Through Dialogue

By simple questions that address what a person already knows, you can lead people to a place at which God's Spirit can confirm Truth to their spirits. The goal is for people to walk away from your conversation thinking Jesus is a viable option. The dialogue below is an example of how I witness. All of it can be done without a Bible. But a Christian of any maturity can find applicable scriptures if he should choose to do so. Many such scriptures can be found in the previous chapters. However, use the kernel of Truth in the scripture without quoting it or saying, "The Bible says. . . ," because using the Bible early in your conversation can give people the idea that you are proselytizing or trying to convert them, and they are not ready for that.

Three cautions:

1) Avoid the temptation to memorize the following dialogue. Our culture likes to have a methodology, seven easy points, a system to follow. However, if you memorize all this, people will feel like they are in a monologue, not a dialogue. But you may wish to master the logical progression of the example.

2) Avoid introducing Jesus too soon. (As I did with the Chinese doctors, you can explain the love of Jesus without saying *Jesus* yet.)

3) As you consider how to begin your dialogue, ask God for discernment. Sometimes God will show you a hurting heart or someone who needs to be cheered up. Listen carefully to the person you are conversing with. Once you understand where a person is, the Spirit will

tell you how to begin. You can probably pick up a cue from the person as to where to start. Some options for getting into dialogue are:
- Start the way I began with the Chinese doctors (see chapter one).
- Begin with the universality of love and how we don't love perfectly.
- Begin with the universality of the Law of karma and how only perfect love could fulfill it, yet no one can love perfectly.
- Or start as follows:

Q: Are you the Creator or the creation?
A: Creation
Q: Do you have to prove it?
A: No.
Q: Then how do you know?
A: That's just the way it is.
Q: Have you ever sinned?
[If "sin" is too sensitive a word, try "missing the Mark" or "bad karma" or "failing to live up to being as good as God."]
A: If they say no, point out that selfishness, anger toward a family member, deceit, etc. are sinful behaviors.
Q: Can you live perfectly and love perfectly as God is perfect?
Or: Can you keep the Law perfectly?
A: No.
Q: Why?
A: Because I am not God.
[Point out that we cannot live perfectly, for we are the creation, not the Creator.]
Q: Did God know this before He created us?
A: Yes.
[Define the love of God. Perfect love would not murder, lie, cheat, or hate. We know that, because God's image is written on every

heart. That image is the universal moral Law.]
- Q: That Law, is it for God or people?
- A: For people.
- Q: Must the Law be fulfilled?

    [There are a variety of ways to ask this. Your goal is to communicate clearly to the person you're talking to. Here are some possibilities:

    Is it true that "what goes around comes around"?
    Do we reap what we sow?
    Are there consequences for what we say or do?
    Must the Law of karma be fulfilled? Or must the cycle be completed?]

- A: [If they say, "No," point out that the result of that is chaos. It is Law that brings order and predictability to our world, preventing chaos. If they say, "Yes," point out that we have already said we cannot satisfy the Law's requirements. The result of not keeping the Law is sin. And the wages of sin is death.]
- Q: Can you forgive your own sin; if you are the cause can you erase the effect?
- A: No.
- Q: So if you die, will you die with your sin?
- A: Yes.
- Q: Is sin for heaven or hell?
- A: Not heaven.
- Q: If someone could erase the effect of your bad karma (your sin), would that be a good thing?
- A: Yes.
- Q: But you can't forgive your own sin or keep the Law perfectly. Who can?
- A: Only God can forgive sin or keep the Law.

Then explain the love of God as shown in Jesus Christ fulfilling the Law, satisfying its requirements. The Law is written in every heart. Since only God can keep this Law, God must become man to do for man what man cannot do for himself.

This model may not work with everyone. That's why you need to have an understanding of its logical progression so the Holy Spirit can bring it out of you. Sometimes you'll get stumped, but don't end the conversation. Just say, "Let me think about that." Listen for references to Law. You can then springboard to love and the fact that love is seen through Jesus, God acting in human affairs to redeem us for violating the requirements of the moral Law. The gospel is simply God's love making itself known through Jesus Christ.

New from best-selling author Karyn Henley!

Love Trumps Karma
Uncovering the Truth You <u>Know</u> You Know

For Ages 12-19. Based on *The Truth You <u>Know</u> You Know*, by N. Kenneth Rideout

Your Hindu, Buddhist, and New Age friends seem kinder, more accepting and generous, and less judgemental than some Christians you know. And Christians are supposed to be the most loving people on earth! Go figure! Your friends talk about good karma, bad karma. They're right. They've got karma, You've got karma. Like it or not, we've all got karma.

But that's not all we have in common. In *Love Trumps Karma*, you will uncover what we all know we <u>know</u> and find out what you *really* believe and why.

Available online at www.LoveTrumpsKarma.com